FAT CATS AND DEMOCRATS

OTHER BOOKS BY THE AUTHOR

Who Rules America?, 1967
C. Wright Mills and the Power Elite, 1968 (co-editor)
The Higher Circles, 1970

FAT CATS
AND
DEMOCRATS

THE ROLE OF THE BIG RICH
IN THE PARTY OF THE COMMON MAN

G. WILLIAM DOMHOFF

PRENTICE-HALL, INC.
Englewood Cliffs, N.J.

TO FERDINAND LUNDBERG

*Fat Cats and Democrats: The Role of The Big Rich in The
Party of The Common Man*
By G. William Domhoff
Copyright © 1972 by G. William Domhoff
All rights reserved. No part of this book may be
reproduced in any form or by any means, except
for the inclusion of brief quotations in a review,
without permission in writing from the publisher.
Printed in the United States of America
Prentice-Hall International, Inc., London
Prentice-Hall of Australia, Pty. Ltd., North Sydney
Prentice-Hall of Canada, Ltd., Toronto
Prentice-Hall of India Private Ltd., New Delhi
Prentice-Hall of Japan, Inc., Tokyo

Library of Congress Cataloging in Publication Data

Domhoff, G   William.
  Fat cats and Democrats

  Bibliography: p.
  1. Democratic Party. 2. Elections—U. S.—
Campaign funds. 3. Capitalists and financiers—U. S.
4. Upper classes—U. S. I.   Title.
JK2317. 1972.D64   329.3'025   78–38791
ISBN 0-13-308171-0

PREFACE

This book starts with the assumption that candidates in major elections need a large amount of money. This does not mean other factors are unimportant in political campaigns, but it does mean many primary and general election campaigns are impossible without a certain minimum level of financial backing that often runs into millions of dollars.

Systematic sociological research on large campaign donors is difficult because donors and their donations are not always faithfully recorded. Thus I feel more tentative about some of the assertions in this book than I did in my previous studies of the American power structure, *Who Rules America?* and *The Higher Circles.*

Not every piece of information in this book will be up-to-the-minute in its accuracy. People change jobs, retire, or die; corporations get bought and sold. Some people even change political allegiances. What the book should make clear are the broad outlines of Democratic Party financial support.

I have chosen not to encumber the text with extensive footnote references. Essential sources are covered, however, in a Bibliographic Essay at the end.

Many people were essential to the research that went into this book. In particular, I want to thank Herbert E. Alexander of the Citizens' Research Foundation, who allowed me to use his impressive material on campaign finance and gave generously of his time; Bob Sherrill of *The Nation*, who helped me obtain interviews in Washington and the South, and gave me many good ideas; and Ferdinand Lundberg, author of *The Rich and the Super-Rich*, who provided me with many leads and reading suggestions in letters and conversations. Materials and suggestions provided by Paul Booth, Philip Burch, Jr., Murray Frost, Stanley Hopper, James Weinstein, and Maurice Zeitlin also were of great use.

The book would not have been possible without the detailed and painstaking efforts of student research assistants Connie Anthony, Leslie Gray, Andrea Hoover, Allan Hunter, Craig Kubey, Sonné Lemke, Lisa McAllister, Sharon Moss, Donn Rogosin, Peter Spofford, and Margie Waldo, all of whom spent many hours reading microfilm and searching through biographical reference sources.

Two members of the staff at the University of California, Santa Cruz, were especially helpful to this research: Joan Hodgson of Interlibrary Loan, who helped obtain many books, journals, and dissertations, and Helen Sherra of the Social Sciences Division, who made sure I was properly staffed and budgeted.

My thanks also to the many people—journalists, scholars, lawyers, and political activists—who allowed me to interview them in pursuit of material for this book. I will not attempt to name them here, especially because some of them prefer anonymity, but I am sure many of them will recognize the great help they gave me.

Colleagues who read the final manuscript have saved me from many sins, both substantive and stylistic. These friendly critics include political scientists Herbert E. Alexander, Philip Burch, Jr., Douglas Fox, Harry Scoble, and Benjamin W. Smith; sociologists Chandler Davidson and

Richard Hamilton; and anthropologist Sam Stanley. Bob Sherrill checked the chapters on the South and the liberals, making many useful comments.

Stylistically, my most careful and critical readers were Peter Clecak of The Program in Comparative Culture at the University of California, Irvine, Ferdinand Lundberg, Mickey Flacks, and Judy Domhoff. Peter restrained me from my worst clichés and rhetorical flourishes (in addition to including many substantive suggestions), and Ferdinand tried to pump life into my academic prose. The readability of the book has improved greatly thanks to them.

I also am very grateful to five of my friends in the sociology department at the University of California, Santa Barbara—Dick Flacks, Dave Gold, Milt Mankoff, Harvey Molotch, and John Sonquist—for a pleasant and stimulating visiting year in their department in 1970–71, during which much of this book was researched and written.

As so often in the past, the final manuscript was typed by Mrs. Charlotte Cassidy of Cowell College. I cannot thank her enough for keeping a careful watch on my grammar and my spelling, especially my spelling of people's names. I have had virtually no complaints since she took over this assignment.

A word of thanks, too, to my editor at Prentice-Hall, Michael Hunter, who took a chance on this book when it was only an idea, and remained calm and reassuring while it was being written.

The book owes its title to Judy Domhoff, who is fast becoming an expert in this department.

G. William Domhoff
Cowell College
University of California, Santa Cruz

CONTENTS

1

ONE BIG PROPERTY PARTY

THE SAVIOR OF THE COMMON MAN?

"The Democratic Party is great because it looks out for the little man. We're the party of the common man."

Such was the proud boast of a grand old political warhorse, the late Emma Guffey Miller of Pennsylvania, in the spring of 1969. Her words fell upon the ears of loyal Democrats during one of the many Jefferson-Jackson dinners at which party leaders around the country pass the money-raising hat each year. But they could have been uttered by just about any Democrat, for if there is one thing Democrats love to claim, it is that they are the party of the common man.

The other side of this ornate claim, of course, is that the bad Republicans are the party of bad big business. And it is true that most wealthy men, especially bankers and industrialists, are deep-dyed Republicans. Year after year, the same Socially Registered bluebloods appear on the GOP's financial rolls. Not surprisingly, then, the Republicans have much more money to play with than the Democrats, outspending them, on the average, on a six-to-four or seven-to-three basis. It is not hard, therefore, for many people to believe that the Republicans are the special errand boys of the super-rich.

But what about the Democrats? Are they really the party of the common man? Or could it be that the relatively few large contributors who are in the Democratic Party dominate it just as thoroughly as the wealthy Republicans dominate their party?

THE PURPOSE OF THIS BOOK

The purpose of this book is to examine the rich men who support the Democratic Party in order to show that their presence and activities contradict the image of the Democrats as the party of the common man. I will attempt to demonstrate that the party is in fact dominated at its most crucial points by various cliques of fat cats who have spun a nationwide network of social and business connections. They are not quite the same multimillionaires who prevail financially in the grand old Republican Party, and they are not usually as wealthy as their Republican counterparts, but they are extremely well-heeled nonetheless.

There are few members of American academia who can bring themselves to believe that the United States is run by a power elite made up of multimillionaires and their hired executives. Many of their scholarly hesitations are centered on certain widely held illusions about the Democrats and, indeed, about the political process in general.

One such notion is the common-man image of the Democratic Party. After studying voting patterns and opinion polls on party affiliation, thereby learning that most manual workers and blacks register as Democrats and that most coupon clippers and professionals are Republicans, they are prepared to agree with those who would claim that only the Republicans are dominated by the wealthy few.

Another image that keeps academicians from accepting the power-elite theory is the seeming fragmentation of the political parties, and particularly of the Democratic Party. According to this view, each state party is quite separate. Furthermore, the "party" that goes into action in each state is different at the presidential, state, and local levels.

How could a power elite dominate a fragmented party which relies in great measure on black and white workers for its support? The answer is to be found in the tightly knit group of people who decide which candidates will be financed at the various levels of the party. Revealing that the same financial network stands behind the party at its several levels in major states should go a long way toward dispelling objections based on voting patterns and the fragmentation of the party. In this day and age, few candidates get anywhere without big money—really big money.

THE IMPORTANCE OF FAT CATS

The fat cats who contribute $500 or more to individual candidates do not own the party lock, stock, and barrel. They do, though, have a dominant interest. Labor unions

provide as much as twenty to twenty-five percent of the
war chest in some states, racketeers and gangsters—some
of whom are amazingly intimate with respectable Democratic fund raisers—provide ten to fifteen percent in certain metropolitan areas(and perhaps more in Chicago and
Nevada), and little people from the middle classes pick
up about fifteen percent of the tab for elections at all
levels. When all these other contributions to the pot are
acknowledged, however, it is still corporate moneymen
who make the big difference.

They are the ones who raise the bulk of Democratic
funds for presidential elections. They serve as the gilded
bagmen for important campaigns at state and local levels,
even tapping the resources of wealthy Republican friends
who like a particular Democratic candidate or want to
hedge their bets. It is checkbook Democrats who sponsor
testimonial dinners where unrecorded donations can be
made by corporations and their lobbyists. Fat cats provide various free services on the sly—such as free mailings,
free telephones, campaign workers who are on their company payroll, and use of the company airplane. And it is
the heftiest of fat cats who make big loans to the candidate at crucial moments in the campaign.*

Even more importantly, it is these cliques of rich friends
who raise a majority of the funds for primaries at all levels
of government, and it is in primaries that the overly liberal candidates they oppose are usually eliminated from
consideration. Fat cats, then, have a dominant interest
even though it is not always a majority one.

This creates no problem for these savvy gentlemen,

---

* In 1968 a mere forty-three people lent Hubert Humphrey at least $3.1
million, and perhaps as much as $5.9 million, for his last-minute TV blitz.

for they have grown accustomed to controlling corporations with as little as five to ten percent of the stock, where the trick is in keeping the rest of the stock divided into such little holdings that no one else can put together a commanding position. The forty to sixty percent financial stake of fat cats in the Democratic Party has been more than sufficient for their purposes. Some divisions or subsidiaries of the party may get out of hand occasionally, and there are parts of the enterprise that are fairly independent. The following chapters will show, however, that the party as a whole stays within the confines dictated by its financial masters. As the Big Daddy of California Democrats, Jesse Unruh, likes to remind the faithful, money is the mother's milk of politics.

Although the fat cats are indispensable, it should be emphasized that they do not have to strain themselves financially in being so. Most of them spend more in a year on clothes or horses or dogs or servants than they do on politics. Their domination of American politics comes surprisingly cheap. The agitation of the sixties didn't even begin to shift upper-class expenditures from personal consumption to a group-wide defense of the system of swindle and subsidy that sustains them so handsomely. Most members of the higher circles do not even appear on lists of donors who give $500 or more to either party. Even allowing for the considerable error present in such lists, this would suggest that the American upper class as a whole has vast financial reserves to throw into any political battles that are really threatening it. Until such a challenge comes along, politics will remain the hobby or preoccupation of a few cliques and families within the privileged class, cliques and families seeking personal aggrandizement or special favors from the government.

THE MOTIVES OF FAT CATS

What do fat cats want (and usually get) for their money? The general, academic answer is that their desires vary, as is usually the case with any collection of human beings. We can immediately become more specific, however, by saying that what most of them want has to do with their own financial self-interest.

Sometimes what the fat cat wants are contracts for his paving or construction business, like Philadelphia contractor Matt McCloskey, who builds government buildings for his Democratic friends at costs ludicrously beyond original estimates. Sometimes he wants subsidies, like San Francisco Democrat George Killion, whose shipping company gets $32 million a year from the government. Very often the *quid pro quo* is tax exemptions, as in the case of Texas oilmen and urban real-estate developers. There is, too, the need for cooling off restive regulatory agencies and wangling lucrative zoning and building-code violations for real-estate developments.

One of the most important considerations that can make a taproot Democrat out of a wealthy man is a foreign policy that encourages overseas corporate expansion and protects foreign investments that already exist. What is required here is first of all a fairly general policy position, what the heavies in the corporate castles call a proper atmosphere for doing business. The late Democratic corporation lawyer Dean Acheson of the Washington law factory of Covington and Burling, who also served as Secretary of State under Truman, spoke for a great many of his clients and friends when he remarked in 1947: "We cannot go through another ten years like the ten years at the end of the twenties . . . without having the most far-reaching consequences upon our economic and social system. . . . When we look at the problem, we may say it is a problem of markets. . . . We have to see that what the country produces is used and is sold under financial arrangements which makes its production possible. . . . You must look to foreign markets."

Another gold-plated Democrat who speaks for these foreign policy needs is Averell Harriman of the private banking firm of Brown Brothers, Harriman. He had this to say about his conversion to the Democrats in 1928, at a time when he was involved in German zinc mines, Polish iron mines, and, until disagreements arose, Soviet manganese mines:

> I was a good, hard-shelled Republican until 1928. That year I voted for Al Smith against Hoover for several reasons. I thought Republican isolationism was disastrous. I thought the Wilsonian policy of supporting the League of Nations was essential. . . . I also knew that we could not continue to lend money abroad and expect to be repaid unless we changed our tariff policies.

But not all motives for giving can be traced to the desire for profits. There are two other kinds of important Democratic fat cats: those who want to turn their money into status and prestige, and those who are sentimental liberals who want to see a more humane society, which usually means in practice some expansion of civil rights and more reliable welfare measures for the bottom layers of society. Most prominent among the status seekers are newly moneyed Jews and Catholics who are snubbed by wealthy Protestants. The most unexpected group among the liberals, who certainly include a great many Jews, are a handful of well-fixed maverick patricians who have deserted the stodgy Republican atmosphere that envelops most of their peers.

A FEW WORDS ABOUT THE REPUBLICAN PARTY

The Republican Party will appear only from time to time in this narrative, and then merely to show how the Democrats work hand in glove with wealthy Republicans on certain very critical issues. But it is worthwhile to say a few words about the GOP, for it does after all represent the other half of a two-party system that cannot be understood without comprehending the fact that the two parties interact.

What can be said of substance about the Republicans in a capsule? Actually, everything that needs to be said, for the party is much simpler than the sprawling Democratic Party apparatus and ultimately less effective because of its ineptitude in time of economic crisis, its lack of leaders who can relate to the discontents of white ethnics and blacks on the lower rungs of the social ladder, and because of the disappearance of the rural America that once produced so many Republicans. Here then are the generalizations that encompass the Republican Party:

　　1. The Republicans are obviously the preferred party of the American upper crust, for perhaps eighty to ninety percent of the non-Southern members of this tiny privileged group are registered Republicans.

　　2. Compared to the Democrats, the white elephant party is fabulously rich and very well organized.

　　3. The party wins—which of late decades is not

very often—for four reasons. First, it has more money to spend on campaigns. Second, it obfuscates, confuses, and distorts issues with pietistic, nationalistic, and demagogic appeals. That is, like any conservative party in a system where the people can vote, it hides its nature even more than the middle-of-the-road party. Third, the super-wealthy and mildly well-to-do who are its primary backers are more likely to vote than the "ethnic" Americans who are the major constituencies of the Democratic Party. Finally, Republicans sometimes win because many lower-middle and working-class Protestants succumb to their prejudices and to nationalistic rhetoric, and vote with the rich Anglo-Saxons rather than the black and ethnic Americans with whom they share the lower levels of the American income hierarchy. Not all white Protestants fall into this trap, but enough do to give the GOP an occasional victory.

4. Another characteristic of the Republican Party is that it has middle-of-the-road and conservative wings, which might more accurately be called conservative and neanderthal. The conservative Republicans are by and large wealthier and more internationally based in their business connections than the neanderthals, but the presence among the Stone Age true believers of super-rich families like the Milbanks, Pews, Millikens, and du Ponts should not be overlooked. It is the function of the wily conservatives among Republicans to accommodate the reactionaries just enough to keep them from forming an ultra-conservative party, just as it is the task of the wealthy moderate Democrats to assimilate or crush any sanguine liberals who try to stray through the left boundary of the sacred two-party system.

So much for pontifical generalizations, but it also should be said that the Republicans would, if left to themselves,

destroy the economic system that overrewards them in
spite of their shortsightedness and WASPish ethnic arro-
gance. Due in particular to the need to appease the
ghoulish tendencies of the du Ponts, Pews, and petty
rich in small towns, the party forgets nothing and
learns nothing. The administration of Calvin Coolidge—
in highly mythologized form, of course—remains the ideal
for the typical stalwart of the latter-day GOP.

But it is not only economically that the Republican vo-
taries of the dollar would almost surely wreck their own
system. The plain truth is that they cannot relate personally to the heterogeneous American masses. Certainly not
to the Jews, who are excluded from gentile clubs and corporations with a zeal somewhat shocking to the innocent.
Certainly not to the poor, whom they believe to be in-
herently lazy and stupid, not superexploited, and toward
whom their condescension is obvious. Certainly not to the
long-dispossessed blacks, although some prep schools are
now admitting a few so the boys and girls of the highest
echelons can get used to being around them. And not to
the Catholic ethnic groups that predominate in the blue-
collar class, for these Republicans are above all else Protestant and North European and ill at ease with people they
see as foreigners. And certainly not to the long-haired
and pot-smoking among the younger generation, many of
whom are self-made outcasts precisely because they reject what they regard as the plastic and chrome-plated
phoniness of Republican suburbs. Which doesn't leave
much but other white Protestants for the Republicans, as
voting pattern studies indicate. No wonder GOP candidates rely on stage-managed TV and other media that
keep people at a distance. Republicans are not only
wooden nickels. They are also wooden Indians.

Is there anything nice that can be said about the Republicans? Well, it is true that their bark is often worse than their bite. So far they have managed to pull back at the last minute from indulging their worst inclinations. Their business caution often leads them to do less political harm than they'd like. And the far-right clique does have the virtue of being somewhat isolationist, which keeps the party from being as imperialistic and war-minded as the Democrats. (Unfortunately, this isolationist tendency is often nullified by bellicose patriotism; instead of pulling out of "Democratic" wars like Vietnam, which the ultra-conservatives by and large opposed, they insist upon the fantasy of quick and easy military victories by such expedients as the use of "tactical" nuclear weapons.)

There *are* civilized people among the party's more moderate leaders. However, to mention other than obvious examples like Pete McCloskey would be risky for fear one or two of them might be overlooked. It's just that the good guys count for little within the party, and have so little sway over the upper-middle-class mélange of managers, engineers, physicians, and dentists to which the party looks for its support.*

The Republican Party, then, is a spectacular mess when it comes to meeting the crying needs of most Americans. Its coterie of grim public relations men and overly smooth salesmen merely go through the motions of the democratic process. The razzle-dazzle is over in the Democratic Party, where a leadership coalition of wealthy Jewish businessmen, reactionary Southerners, clever corporation lawyers,

---

* On May 1, 1971, the chief of the primitive Republicans in California, a forty-seven-year-old mechanical engineer from Santa Barbara, announced that Nixon had turned "socialistic."

and wealthy Protestant mavericks clumsily embrace each
other while at the same time mollifying a constituency of
blacks, browns, Catholics, middle-class Jews, Southerners,
and well-educated do-gooders. The Democratic Party is
truly an amazing phenomenon, more akin to a circus jug-
gling act than a political organization. It makes the Republican Party look like the dull, cash-on-the-barrelhead
outfit that it is.

SOURCES OF INFORMATION ON FAT CATS

Neither Republicans nor Democrats go out of their way
to advertise their childlike dependency on the check-
books of the corporate rich. Tedious detective work is required even to begin connecting the tangled pipelines
through which political money is pumped. Systematic research, as opposed to the stringing together of anecdotes,
is in its preliminary stages on this neglected topic.

The first and most important method of finding and
identifying Democratic fat cats has been official campaign records. For all the weaknesses these records have,
and they are countless, they are the best possible starting
point. Many of these lists have been compiled by Herbert
E. Alexander of the Citizens' Research Foundation, an
organization specializing in the study of campaign finance. Other telltale traces are preserved in the records
of congressional hearings. Using both of these sources,
we have obtained lists for every presidential election campaign from 1936 through 1968. Guided by these lists, we
then used every available biographical source to find out
about the social and economic connections of the largest
and most faithful Democratic supporters. Out of this information, and especially the more complete information
for the sixties, we slowly pieced together the shadowy

webs and networks that stand behind the Democratic Party.

Campaign lists are not ideal sources of information. For one thing, they probably understate what the major fat cats actually contribute; there are many ways of disguising contributions—by giving cash, by giving through intermediaries, and by giving to state and local fund raising committees in states where political donations need not be reported. For another thing, the lists do not include a great many of the weightiest donors because both major parties have been lax in the recording of donations. And they are worthless for states where there are no reporting laws or where the feeble existing laws are not enforced. This nonreporting problem applies particularly to the South, and the South is an important part of the Democratic story. We thus had to turn to other sources for information on the ubiquitous moneymen.

One such source was a questionnaire sent to political reporters for major newspapers around the country. Although the percentage of returns was not large, a number of prominent fat cats were discovered, particularly for the Southern states. We also sent a questionnaire to all Republican national committeemen and committeewomen, and to Republican state chairmen, in the hope that they might know the enemy better than the enemy knows itself. Returns from this source were less significant. Many of these misguided worthies tend to believe, contrary to all published evidence, that organized labor is the major source of funds for the Democrats.

Another source of information on the fat cats was interviews. Relatively informal, unstructured interviews were held with journalists, academics, political operatives, and fat cats themselves in New York, Washington, Chicago, San Francisco, and Los Angeles. Numerous telephone interviews also were conducted, particularly with people in the Southern states. All told, there were about seventy-five interviews.

Interviews have their uses. They are especially helpful in testing the ideas about interconnections, ideas that have been developed from published sources. However, interviews are by no means the final answer. It is astonishing, for example, how many supposedly knowledgeable people have very little comprehension of the financing of the Democratic Party. It is also disconcerting that many of the alleged insiders to whom I was directed were only repeating what they've read, and what they've read usually has its ultimate source in the fine work of Herbert E. Alexander at the Citizens' Research Foundation. Then there is the problem of the people who will not talk, or who will only talk about trivial things. One Wall Street investment banker wouldn't tell me the names of the other Democrats in his firm; he thought that was "too personal." Published sources, then, are usually more useful than interviews, although interviews help develop new leads and confirm guesses.

No single source of information—campaign records, questionnaires, or interviews—was complete, but all had their uses. Even taken as a whole, they undoubtedly leave large gaps in our full understanding of the financing of the Democratic Party. It is not a subject conducive to punctilious accounting.

SOME HISTORICAL PERSPECTIVE

A great deal of the preparation for this book went into historical study of the Democratic Party. Although only small amounts of that history will be brought to bear in this sociological inquiry into the present-day financing of the party, it did lend a perspective of timelessness to the whole venture. For the same themes appear with monotonous regularity throughout American political history. The times are always perilous; the particular election in question is the worst crisis the country ever has faced. When we learn from newspaper and magazine columnists that the 1964 campaign was a possible turning point, or that 1972 will be the most important campaign in 20 or 50 or 150 years, we are impressed or frightened only if we forget what has been written by political commentators every four years since the Republic began.

Then there's always the reform Democrat or independent Democrat who is fighting corruption or the big bad political machine. Things will never be the same after he is elected, except that they always are. Also sure to appear quite regularly is the hardy notion that the party has outlived its usefulness and is disintegrating. The imminent death of the Democrats and the formation of a new party is deduced from one theory or another about every decade. At the same time as the burial is being prepared, however, there are others who have hope for the rebirth of the party because the idealism and enthusiasm of the virginal new generation now presumably invigorating the party will revive the faded American dream—except the younger generation grows old and turns out to be as self-seeking and corruptible as the previous generation.

Reading through mountains of such literary hysteria has made me skeptical about the supposedly unprecedented peril of the seventies—or even the eighties. At the least it makes me suspect that present-day political observers predicting disaster have no more solid basis for their fantasies than previous apocalyptic thinkers; it will be pure luck if they happen to be right. With so many great experts predicting so many different things, surely one of them will someday "predict" the future by sheer chance. Most didn't during the sixties, however. Johnson abdicate? Nixon make a comeback? Obviously impossible.

Political nonsense, then, appears as each election approaches, and it never changes. The basic point about American political campaigns is that they are ninety-eight percent stale baloney. They are rhetorical outpourings in which crisis and impending doom are our visualized fate. It is amazing that the distracted American electorate occasionally sees through the smog and confusion long enough to pick the lesser of the two obvious evils.

THE PROPERTY PARTY

In the few words about the Republican Party it was noted that the Democrats must be considered as part of a two-party system. Actually, this is to a great extent an illusion of the intellectual elite that huddle around such ideology factories as Harvard, Yale, Princeton, and Stanford. A better statement of the situation is that of an academic outsider, Ferdinand Lundberg, author of *America's Sixty Families* (1937) and *The Rich and The Super-Rich* (1968), who points out that what we have is a one-party system with two branches. That one party, Lundberg announces, should be called the Property Party:

> The United States can be looked upon as having, in effect, a single party: the Property Party. This party can be looked upon as having two subdivisions: The Republican Party, hostile to accommodating adjustments (hence dubbed "Conservative") and the Democratic Party, of recent

decades favoring such adjustments (hence dubbed "Liberal").

Lundberg is not entirely alone in this insight. It is just that you have to look for it through heavy disguise and opaque language in the scholarly literature. Rarely does an academic treatise reveal how the American Constitution was carefully rigged by the noteholders, land speculators, rumrunners, and slaveholders, who were the Founding Fathers, so that it would be next to impossible for upstart dirt farmers and indebted masses to challenge the various forms of private property held by these well-read robber barons. Through this Constitution the over-privileged attempted to rule certain topics out of order for proper political discussion. To bring these topics up in polite company was to invite snide invective, charges of personal instability, or financial ruin.

Fundamentals about the protection and enhancement of the private properties of the high and mighty were set in concrete at the beginning of the Republic; they have been essential to the functioning of the "two-party" system ever since. This acceptance of basic principles explains what some find a remarkable phenomenon—that a "loyal opposition" has been able to grow up in America. When it is understood that the loyal opposition has been led by such men of breeding and propertied background as Thomas Jefferson, Franklin D. Roosevelt, and John F. Kennedy, men who never publicly questioned the fundamental assumptions, perhaps it is not such a miracle to behold after all. For all the high-flown rhetoric of the reactionary Republicans, it is a little hard for most members of the upper class to believe that a deep-rooted patrician like Franklin Roosevelt was contemplating revolution.

Since the Democrats and Republicans are but two branches of the One Big Party, both are underwritten by the large property holders in several ways that are often overlooked in discussions narrowly focused on the financing of individual candidates. To begin with, the national conventions of the two parties are subsidized by grants of from $300,000 to $1 million by the business community of the host city. The influx of politicos is considered by the always-friendly business leaders to stimulate spending within their city, and the subsidy permits a tax deduction besides because it is a business expense. It seems unlikely, however, that political conventions are such good business that the local millionaires would give several hundred thousand dollars to bring the Democrats to town were they an antiproperty party.

Another business subsidization of the two parties comes through expensive ads in the party convention programs. Since this too is "advertising," it is, of course, a tax-deductible business expense; the corporate chieftains would insist they have no other motive than making their products known to office-seekers and party functionaries. In 1936, the year the ultra-conservative rich were most disenchanted with the Democrats because of various New Deal innovations, some staunch Republicans were nonetheless among those who diplomatically allowed their corporations to buy $385,000 worth of ads in the less-than-engrossing *Book of the Democratic Convention;* another $250,000 came to the Democrats from selling copies of the book to corporations. In 1964, a banner year, the Democrats helped pay for their convention with $1.5 million raised from ad sales.

One of the nicest and least known favors granted by the corporate rich to both the Republican and Democratic branches of their Big Property Party is a special discount for debts piled up by losing candidates. Hotels, airlines, and telephone companies extend tens of thousands of dollars in credit to candidates of both parties, then settle with the loser at a cut-rate price—with thirty-three cents on the dollar being a fairly typical figure.

When these and lesser gratuities—such as free cars for big shots at conventions—are added in, the fat cats' contribution to the One Big Property Party is even larger than it seems on first glance. "The full extent of services contributed by American business as promotional activities during a national political convention is enormous," write John F. Bibby and Herbert E. Alexander. "When this evidence of corporate services in kind is coupled with the cash contributions business concerns have made either in the form of gifts to host committees or program advertising space, it is obvious that political parties—at least in their convention activities—have become heavily dependent upon business largesse."

A Property Party with two branches is one of the neatest devices ever stumbled upon by rich men determined to stay on top. It gives them a considerable flexibility, allowing them to form temporary coalitions with different elements of the underlying population as the occasion demands. It allows them to "throw the rascals out" without themselves becoming too closely identified with any one set of rascals. It allows most of them to stay aloof from mere "partisan" political battles, only to descend on the scene from time to critical time as high-minded civic leaders concerned with the "public interest." Or they can pose as "good government" citizens who encourage "worthwhile" candidates in both parties, or who even finance both candidates for an office at the same time, for they "believe in" the two-party system and want to support it.

So one is not surprised that many wealthy businessmen

play down their party affiliation, that "nonpartisan" multimillionaires join committees to support the "best man," that Democratic and Republican money collectors can join together on numerous "bipartisan" committees for the national good, that many corporations and law firms have representatives on both sides of the political fence, and that corporate executives give their easily-earned monies to Republicans in one race and Democrats in another. Anything for "sound" government.

THE IMPORTANCE OF THE DEMOCRATS

It is not sufficient to say the two parties agree on Big Property fundamentals and are dominated by overpriced men whose primary concern is more and more corporate profits. There are some differences in the two political parties—in their constituencies, in their programs, in their style and tone, and even, to some extent, in their fat cats. It does make a cash difference to a great many people which one triumphs in elections. The coalition which is the Republican Party puts even more tax burdens on the consumer while neglecting social services and trying to undermine organized labor. The coalition which is the Democratic Party, even with the albatross of its Southern faction, provides a friendlier climate for its black and working-class supporters. So the Democrats probably are better for the common man.

But not much better. Despite the social and economic hardships suffered by hundreds of millions of Americans over the past one hundred years, the power elite have been able to contain demands for a steady job, fair wages, good pensions, and effective health care within very modest limits compared to other highly developed Western countries. One of the most important factors in maintaining those limits has been the Democratic Party. The party dominates the left alternative in this country, and the sophisticated rich want to keep it that way. Democrats are not only attractive to the working man, but vital to the wealthy, too, precisely because they are the branch of the Property Party that to some extent *accommodates* labor, blacks, and liberals, but at the same time hinders genuine economic solutions to age-old problems.

ORGANIZED LABOR AND THE DEMOCRATS

One of the prevalent fantasies about the Democrats is that they are dominated by organized labor. Although labor unions are essential to the Democrats, providing big financial and organizational support in some cities (especially Detroit), they are clearly second stringers who have even less influence than would be expected on the basis of their drudgery for the party in getting out the vote.

Why, then, is the image of labor domination so widespread? It is the standard campaign rhetoric of Republicans, who use it to scare their nonunionized constituency of white-collar workers and professionals. Again, labor domination of the Democratic Party is one of the stock-in-trade fantasies of some super-rightists who really believe organized labor is on the upswing in America despite the relatively small percentage of the work force that is unionized. They cannot comprehend that the unions are struggling to hold their own. Few understand clearly that union leaders have entered into an uneasy bargain with the corporate rich, helping to keep the labor force in line at home and cooperating in CIA labor union operations around the world in exchange for union recognition, periodic wage hikes tied to productivity gains, and the right to help determine working conditions. Still another reason the power of organized labor is often overestimated is that many labor leaders exaggerate the importance of their role. They like to be puffed up as Spokesmen and Statesmen—their status is enhanced and they look good to the people who pay the dues. They are not about to help their critics in the rank and file by admitting they are like office boys compared to the free-wheeling fat cats who dominate the party of the common man.*

AN OUTLINE OF WHAT'S IN STORE

The next chapter will describe the complicated web of finance houses, corporations, and law firms in New York, Texas, California, and major Northern cities that provides the major fund raisers of the Democratic Party. The central role of Jewish businessmen will be stressed, although it will be noted that the few Protestant and Catholic multimillionaires among the Democrats are essential to the legitimation of the party. The ambiguous role of Washington lawyers in blurring party distinctions also will be touched upon.

The third chapter dissects the Democratic Party in

---

* Senator Russell Long, an oil multimillionaire from Louisiana, is among the many who would deny a crucial role to labor money in national politics. "Labor contributions," he said in 1967, "have been greatly exaggerated. It would be my guess that about 95 percent of campaign funds at the congressional level are derived from businessmen. At least 80 percent of this comes from men who could sign a net worth statement exceeding a quarter of a million dollars." As noted earlier, however, labor's contribution to the Democratic Party may be as much as 20 to 25 percent in some states and some elections.

the South. We will see that the businessmen and bankers who dominate the Southern wing of the party are intimately connected with the Northern businessmen essential to the sustenance of the GOP. The historical reasons for the seemingly improbable allegiance of the Southern branch of the upper class to the Democratic Party will be discussed, and the future of the Democratic Party in the South will be suggested.

The fourth chapter will examine the financially blessed liberals who give very large sums to the Democratic Party and to the several organizations that help its liberal wing. The nationwide network of foundations and institutes that the moneyed liberals have created will be unraveled, as will their dual role as innovators and guardians within the power elite.

After this sustained focus on the Democratic fund raisers, the final chapter will blossom into a general discussion of the American political system. It will make a distinction between the candidate-selection process and the policy-formation process, stressing how unimportant the candidate-selection process actually is except in weeding out staunchly principled or otherwise unreliable candidates. The discussion of the policy process will show how top corporate men from both parties join together to develop general policies through a cluster of interlocking foundations, institutes, associations, special commissions, and governmental advisory committees. The role of lobbyists and corporate lawyers in taking care of the needs of specific corporations or industries will be duly chronicled. Not to be overlooked, finally, is the way in which the super-rich of both parties help each other in isolating those candidates who are too liberal or too reactionary.

The inevitable conclusion is that the wealthy few are

firmly in the political saddle despite the existence of an entity billed as the party of the common man. About one percent of the population—a socially interacting upper class whose members go to prep schools, attend debutante balls, join exclusive clubs, ride to hounds, and travel all over the world for business and pleasure—will continue to own sixty to seventy percent of all privately-held corporate wealth and receive twenty-four percent of the yearly national income.

On the other hand, the rest of the American citizenry will continue to pay the lion's share of the taxes and to fight among themselves over the few crumbs that the fat cats can't manage to keep among themselves. Fear of "communism," respect for "experts," reverence for successful corporation-builders, and racial, religious, and ethnic antagonisms among wage earners will continue in all probability to keep the majority of the great unwashed safely divided into warring camps that are unable to collectively challenge their corporate masters.

2

JEWS AND COWBOYS

WALL STREET

Deep in the heart of the New York financial district, a milieu fabled and feared in American hagiography under the designation "Wall Street," there exists a complicated set of familial, social, and business entanglements that form the basis for a network of Democratic Party financial backing that spreads its golden strands throughout the entire United States. This network is especially prominent in the cities and states that are pivotal in determining national control of the party of the common man.

The handful of men in Democratic Central on Wall Street are junior partners in a moneybund that *Fortune* writer T. A. Wise calls "the hard financial core of capitalism in the free world [which] is composed of not more than sixty firms, partnerships, and corporations owned or controlled by some 1,000 men." Along with their Republican superiors and a few confederates in Britain and Western Europe, these Wall Street Democrats help raise, continues Wise, "an estimated 75% of the $40 billion in fresh capital needed each year to fuel the long-term growth of the industrial nations."

Now, Wall Street is clearly a small, intimate place. Every major firm seems to have social, business, or familial connections with the other giants. Especially in the financing of the numerous overseas adventures of American companies, the big financial underwriters appear indiscriminate in the temporary alliances they develop to raise money for a particular corporation. However, there are patterns within Wall Street. Some people do more business with some firms than with others. It is one of these cliques that is at the financial heart of the Democratic Party.

Two major groupings have existed among Wall Street investment bankers for nearly one hundred years. They are the Yankees and the Jews. The Yankees are a set of firms whose founding partners came to Wall Street from New England in the second and third quarters of the nineteenth century. They are the descendants of Puritans, ship captains, Boston merchants, and wealthy New England farmers. They became the financial underwriters and advisers for most of the large banks, railroads, and industrial corporations that grew to prominence after the Civil War and that have dominated the American economy ever since.

First among equals in the Yankee clique is the firm of Morgan, Stanley, the direct heir to the business of J. P. Morgan & Co., which was the driving force behind the organization of U.S. Steel, General Electric, Southern

Railway, and dozens of other blue-chip corporations. Morgan, Stanley is buttressed by such other old respectable investment bankers as First Boston; Kidder, Peabody; and Paine, Webber, Jackson, and Curtis—all with roots in New England soil. However, because several counting houses dominated by Anglo-Saxons from New York, Philadelphia, and one or two other major cities are now part of this clique, it will be referred to as the Anglo-Saxon or gentile investment banking community.

The history of the Jewish investment banking firms is quite different. Most of their founders do not have pedigrees that go back to the founding of the Republic. Instead, they landed in the United States as poor immigrants from Germany and France in the middle of the past century. Most of them started out as impoverished peddlers in the South, the Midwest, and the goldfields of California.

Following their sojourn in the American hinterlands, the most successful of these Jewish immigrants gravitated to Wall Street. With one or two notable exceptions, however, they were not yet wealthy enough when they arrived to finance the burgeoning railroads and manufacturing corporations, which fell solidly into Yankee hands. But they did reach maturity just in time for the growth of light industries and retail businesses in the early years of this century. Less established than the Yankees, they were willing to take a few more risks with these new ventures that were shunned by the now-comfortable rulers of American money. Moreover, many of the new retail businesses coming into their own were owned by other successful Jewish peddlers, so it is not surprising that "Let the Jews have that one" became a common phrase among the intolerant Anglo-Saxon moneychangers.

Thus, for a combination of reasons, Jewish financiers provided much of the nourishment for businesses like mail-order houses, department stores, and movies, while the gentiles tended to concentrate in banking, insurance, and manufacturing. This division of labor still exists to some extent today, although both groups have moved into new opportunities in oil, aerospace, and electronics.

The most important firms within the Jewish banking fraternity are Lehman Brothers; Goldman, Sachs; Carl M. Loeb, Rhoades; Lazard Freres; and Kuhn, Loeb. Each has a slightly different history, and each is more concentrated in some types of business than others. Lehman Brothers, for example, began as a cotton brokerage business in the South, moved into the buying and selling of other basic commodities like grain and sugar when it migrated to New York, and then made its name in the first two decades of this century by financing large retailing businesses in conjunction with Goldman, Sachs, which had begun by making short-term cash loans to small merchants in New York. Lazard Freres on the other hand was begun by French-Jewish immigrants who made their fortunes selling goods to, and performing banking services for, California gold miners. Today it is the investment adviser for some of the largest international companies in the world, such as RCA and ITT, as well as for one of the most important families ever to be involved in the Democratic Party, the Kennedys.

Carl M. Loeb, Rhoades is the infant of the group, dating its birth from 1931 when John L. Loeb, the son of a highly successful business executive, decided to try his hand at investment banking. The company has grown under his iron will to be one of the most potent on Wall Street. (Today, John L. Loeb is the Number One Democratic fund raiser among investment bankers, a job which involves the raising of millions of dollars from his friends, business associates, and clients.)

Kuhn, Loeb, the grandaddy of the five, was the most prominent Jewish investment house of the early twentieth century. Starting earlier than the others in the clique, and having the benefit of partners who came from wealthy families in Germany, its stature was second only to that of J. P. Morgan & Co. in the early financing of railroads. While not as pre-eminent now as in former days, it is still one of the most respected firms on Wall Street.

The firms making up the inner core of the Jewish banking fraternity on Wall Street are no mere collection of names brought together on a list because their founding partners happened to be Jewish. To the contrary, they are intimately related by family and business ties reaching back to the first members of their families to arrive in this country. The intermarriages among families associated with the group defy total schematization. "Today the intermarriage within the crowd presents a design of mind-reeling complexity," says Stephen Birmingham, the author of *Our Crowd,* a tidbit-laden social history of the group's most famous families. "But envision a dewy cobweb in the early morning on a patch of grass. Each drop of dew represents a great private banking house; the radii that fan out are sons and daughters, grandsons and grand-daughters, and the lacy filaments that tie the whole together are marriages."

Lehman relatives alone connect most of the Jewish banking houses into one big family. John L. Loeb of Carl M. Loeb, Rhoades is married to a Lehman. So is Benjamin Buttenwieser, one of the top partners at Kuhn, Loeb. Arthur Altschul of Goldman, Sachs is a close Lehman relative. Gustave Lehmann Levy of that same firm is a more distant relation. No outsiders are sure whether the Bella Lehman married to André Meyer at Lazard Freres is of "the" Lehmans by some distant connection, but blood lines that tie Lehmans to second-tier Jewish banking houses like Hallgarten & Co. and Wertheim & Co. are concretely documented.

The banking crowd, of course, does not discriminate against money made in other endeavors. Joseph F. Cullman, III, of the family that controls Philip Morris, is married to a Lehman. Another Lehman offspring married the scion of General Cigar Company. But Ann Lehman Loeb really struck it rich. She married Edgar Bronfman, son of the wealthiest man in Canada, thanks to Distillers Corporation–Seagrams, Ltd. "Now I know what it feels like to be a poor relation," is the famous remark made by father-in-law John L. Loeb at the wedding.

The examples could go on and on. Kuhns married to Loebs. Schiffs (of Kuhn, Loeb) married to Warburgs (of Kuhn, Loeb). Strauses (of Macy's) merged with Sachses (of Goldman's). Sulzbergers (of *The New York Times*) married to Strauses (again of Macy's). But a halt has to be called somewhere. The marital habits of the Jewish financial aristocracy in America are a study in themselves.

In the present generation many members of this in-group, young adults of the fourth and fifth generation of wealthy Western European Jewish families, are marrying into wealthy families outside the crowd, and only a few from each family are becoming involved in the investment banking business. The five firms of the inner core, however, remain as closely related in business as their founding families are in marriage. They still tend to work together more than they work with firms outside the original clique.

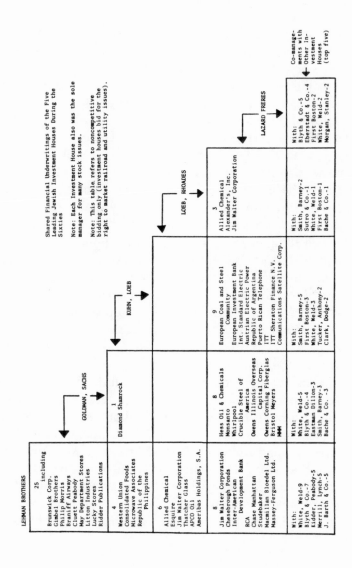

This fact is most readily documented in the accompanying chart, which encompasses some of their business interactions by listing all instances during the sixties where one of these five firms joined with another investment house to sell the new stock issuances of a corporation. In scanning this network, note that few investment houses outside the clique shared as many co-managements of stock issuances with one of the inner five as did one or more of the other four firms within the crowd. The idea of the Jewish banking fraternity as an interrelated club still has a basis in business as well as in social reality.

After all this build-up, it is probably needless to say that it is the Jewish businessmen, not the gentiles, who provide the financial leadership of the Democratic Party on Wall Street, in addition to rendering a number of services and amenities for candidates and officials of the party. For one thing, several families of this group provide the party with some of its biggest contributors and fund raisers. In 1964, for example, various Lehmans are on record for a total of $37,000 to Democratic candidates, and André Meyer of Lazard Freres chipped in with $35,-000 on his own. In 1968, John L. Loeb and his relatives and partners donated $90,500, and Loeb personally lent another $100,000.

Among the most consistent Democratic donors of sizable proportions down through the years have been James Warburg, Edward M. M. Warburg, Mrs. Samuel B. Grimsom, and Dorothy Schiff. All are members of the families around Kuhn, Loeb. And Frederick M. Warburg, one of the managing triumvirate of the firm, gave $11,500 to Democrats in 1968 despite his usual predilection for forward-looking Republicans.

In addition to the essential ingredient of hard cash,

some families of the Jewish banking community provide the party with precious information and expertise on financial and business problems. Thus, André Meyer served on several commissions for President John F. Kennedy, a trust that no doubt built up from Meyer's handling of personal financial matters for Kennedy's father. Harold Linder, a former partner in Carl M. Loeb, Rhoades and the party's largest recorded contributor in 1964 with a ringing $61,000, served the party for seven years as chief of the Export-Import Bank before retiring in 1968. Lehman Brothers sent partner Edward Gudeman to the New Frontier as Under-Secretary of Commerce. Lesser Washington positions were filled in the sixties by Mark Feer of Kuhn, Loeb and Peter Lewis of Lazard Freres.

Then, too, the Jewish banking firms lend the Democratic candidates their respectability and prestige as successful businessmen. Of seven New York investment bankers who signed a "Businessmen for Humphrey-Muskie" ad in the *Wall Street Journal* in 1968, five were from the inner clique—Robert Lehman and George Ball of Lehman Brothers, Sidney Weinberg of Goldman, Sachs, John L. Loeb of Loeb, Rhoades, and André Meyer of Lazard Freres. The only old Democratic standby missing was Benjamin Buttenwieser of Kuhn, Loeb; perhaps he felt restrained because he had been a strong supporter of Eugene McCarthy.

The provision of jobs for footloose Democrats of impeccable connections is another red-carpet service offered by the Jewish banking group. Thus, George Ball, a Washington lawyer and intimate of Adlai Stevenson, left the State Department in 1966 after five years' duty to become one of the senior partners in Lehman Brothers. Henry Fowler, who had been Secretary of the Treasury, found a

new position as one of the top two or three partners at
Goldman, Sachs. C. R. Smith of Texas, president of American Airlines before taking over as boss of the Commerce
Department at the insistence of his friend Lyndon Johnson, joined Lazard Freres after his tour of government
office. So did Frederick V. Deming, who had been an Assistant Secretary of the Treasury.

When it comes to the Democratic Party, however, one
of the most significant facts about this clique of investment bankers is that its members serve as financial underwriters and advisers for other leading Democratic fund
raisers and fat cats—whether Jewish, Catholic, or Texan
—all over the country. Lew Wasserman of MCA (Music
Corporation of America) in Los Angeles, gave Humphrey
at least $54,000 in 1968—MCA does its investment bank-
ing with Lehman Brothers. George Killion of the American
President Lines in San Francisco has been a top Democratic fund raiser in California since the early forties—
APL does its investment banking with Lehman Brothers.

When people think of big Democratic money in Florida,
they think of Jim Walter of the Jim Walter Corporation
—his stock issuances are offered by Leob, Rhoades. Down
Texas way oilman and financier John D. Murchison is
one of the members of the party's major money-raising
organization, the sixty-eighty-man National Finance Council—he does his investment banking with Goldman,
Sachs. Another prominent Texas oil tycoon, Jubal Parten,
a very regular donor of large proportions, does his with
Loeb, Rhoades.

One of the biggest donors to Democratic causes from
the New York area is Mary Lasker, super-wealthy widow
of ad tycoon Albert Lasker—her financial adviser is the
same André Meyer of Lazard Freres who advises the

Kennedys. The two men who have put up the most Democratic money in New Jersey in recent years have been Leon Hess of Amerada-Hess Petroleum and the late Charles Engelhard of Engelhard Industries—both have close ties to Loeb, Rhoades.

Away out in Oregon there is a $438 million company called Evans Products, makers of plywood, precut homes, and bus heaters, among other things. Its president, Monford A. Orloff, is the state's man on the Democrats' National Finance Council. Its investment banker is Goldman, Sachs. One of the members of the National Finance Council from Illinois is Ben Heineman, the chief of Northwest Industries—also a customer of Goldman, Sachs.

By all accounts the most important Democrats in Oklahoma are the Kerrs and McGees of Kerr-McGee Oil Company. This is a $667 million operation which controls twenty-five percent of the country's uranium reserves, thanks in part to the fine footwork of company founder Robert Kerr during his fifteen years in the U.S. Senate. Their investment banker is Lehman Brothers. Kuhn, Loeb plays that role for Phillips Petroleum, another Oklahoma oil giant with officials who raise money for Democratic candidates.

In short, Jewish investment bankers from Wall Street, along with their business clients in major states such as California, Texas, and Illinois, are the members of the corporate community who raise a major portion (the exact percentage would be difficult if not impossible to calculate) of the tens of millions of dollars needed by Democratic presidential, senatorial, and gubernatorial candidates.

Before turning our attention to other aspects of the business clique of which the Jewish investment bankers are an important component, two *crucial caveats* are necessary in talking about them as leading fund raisers within the Democratic Party. For one thing, the partners in the major Jewish investment houses are not exclusively Democrats. In fact, they are predominantly Republican, and many of them are very significant figures within the Republican Party. Lehman partner Lucius Clay, for example, has served as chairman of GOP fund-raising efforts at the national level. Robert Lehman, who was the directing partner until his death in 1969, was an angel to Republicans until the 1964 and 1968 elections. The present lead partner at the firm, Frederick Ehrman, whose family ties in San Francisco connect the firm with the Schwabachers, Koshlands, and other prominent Jewish families of that city, gave the Republicans over $42,000 in 1968.

Gustave Lehmann Levy, the top partner in Goldman, Sachs since the death of Sidney Weinberg in 1969, is a heavy Republican contributor even though he gave $7,000 to LBJ in 1964 and $3,000 to Democrats in 1968. Over at Kuhn, Leob, the pre-eminent John M. Schiff is a Republican regular who gave at least $15,000 in 1952, $18,550 in 1956, $11,500 in 1960, $10,000 in 1964, and $24,500 in 1968.

The major conclusion that clearly emerges from our investigation of the financial contributions of all partners in these firms is that as a group they spread their gifts to candidates in both political parties. Since the gentile financial community is almost exclusively Republican, however, it is the Jewish financiers who by default provide the Democrats with their handful of essential money raisers among the super-wealthy of Wall Street.

Indeed, we found no big Democratic donors among the leading partners of the largest gentile firms. Only two

Anglo-Saxon investment bankers bought a place for themselves in the "Businessmen for Humphrey-Muskie" ad in the *Wall Street Journal*. They were J. Morton Davis of Blair (D. H.) & Company, who also contributed $5,000 to Democrats in 1968, and Paul Miller, president of Drexel Harriman Ripley, Incorporated, who was good for $2,000 in contributions. Taken as a whole, then, investment bankers, whether gentile or Jewish, are overwhelmingly Republican. But, to repeat, those few within the Jewish community who are Democrats have pivotal roles in the funding of that party's candidates.

One other point must be made about the Jewish firms. They now have many non-Jewish partners. For example, Kuhn, Loeb's Thomas A. Kenny is the son of millionaire William F. Kenny, one of the most prominent Catholic backers of Democratic presidential candidate Al Smith in 1928. Another Kuhn, Loeb partner, John B. Ryan, III, is a great-grandson of Thomas Fortune Ryan, the Virginian who took Wall Street by storm in the 1890's and spent millions of dollars on Democratic candidates in the first twenty-eight years of the twentieth century. The same firm also can boast of Thomas E. Dewey, Jr., son of the late Republican nominee for President in 1944 and 1948.

Eugene Black, Jr., son of a Southern-born Democrat prominent in the Rockefellers' Chase Manhattan Bank for many years, is a gentile-in-good-standing at Loeb, Rhoades, as is a former Texas Democrat, Robert B. Anderson. Anderson, in fact, is the Texan who interested his colleague John L. Loeb in becoming active for LBJ in 1964.

The first non-Lehman to become a partner in Lehman Brothers was a gentile from Montana, John Hancock, who was Lehman's man on the boards of such retail giants as

Bond Stores, Jewel Tea, and Kroger Company for many years. He was also a top-level Democratic adviser. Although a strong link between business and politics in his own right, he is best remembered in Democratic history as the right-hand man in political matters to lone-wolf Jewish financier Bernard Baruch. Baruch served as a primary liaison between Wall Street and the Democrats from the inauguration of Woodrow Wilson until the end of the Truman era.

The incorporation of gentiles into their firms differentiates the Jewish investment bankers from the gentiles once again, for it is difficult to find Jewish partners on that side of the fence. This fits the persistent pattern of anti-Semitic discrimination in banking, insurance, and manufacturing enterprises owned and managed by the Episcopalians and Presbyterians who predominate in the American upper class.

Why are the few Democratic fat cats on Wall Street members of the Jewish investment banking community? Several answers to this question will be offered, but they must be postponed until an elaboration of the Jewish-Cowboy business clique allows us to put the question into a larger perspective.

THE JEWISH-COWBOY CLIQUE

To an outsider the corporate community appears monolithic, and well it should, for the similarities in economic interests and life styles among its leaders and beneficiaries far outweigh their personal, religious, and philosophical idiosyncrasies. The interlocking and overlapping of business directorships seems endless, while the sharing of bankers, lawyers, accountants, consultants, and lobbyists among many different corporations makes identifiable patterns seem highly unlikely.

Appearances to the contrary, however, there do persist in attenuated form what economists of a bygone era called "interest groups"—cliques of businessmen, bankers, and lawyers bound together by bonds of friendship, tradition, interlocking directorships, and common business interests that often lead to a lot of mutual backscratching exceptionally lucrative to all concerned.

The Jewish investment bankers on Wall Street are part of—which does not mean in control of—one of the least-known of the interest groups within the big business community. I call this group the Jewish-Cowboy clique because it is a nationwide group with two major components, the Jewish businessmen of New York and the Cowboy oilmen of Texas.

This does not mean, however, that New York-based investment bankers and Texas oilmen join together in managing the affairs of every company that might be considered part of this interest group. Many companies in the group have no Texas leadership. Moreover, other Northern Jewish multimillionaires besides New Yorkers, as well as wealthy Cowboys from other states in the oil regions of the Southwest are also included in the Jewish-Cowboy clique. There are also a few Northern gentiles.

The Jewish-Cowboy business group is not as cohesive as most of the business cliques that have been identified in the past. And members of the group share the leadership of many of their business interests with other large owners, especially the Rockefellers. Despite these disclaimers, however, it is a discernible group within the larger corporate community.

Most vital for our purposes, its members are not quite

as solidly Republican in their political leanings as in the rest of the big business world. That is, many of the companies in the Jewish-Cowboy clique have a small number of prominent Democrats on their boards. These are the men—in addition to the investment bankers already discussed—who raise large campaign war chests for Democratic Party candidates.

It is not easy to demarcate the exact boundaries of an interest group, for important business information is not always available to us. Nor is it easy to present very much detail about an interest group in brief and readable prose form. For these two reasons, I will merely highlight the major business outlines of the Jewish-Cowboy clique, along with presenting a few examples not utilized earlier of prominent Democratic fat cats who are part of it.

Few of the country's major industrial corporations are part of the Jewish-Cowboy clique. Those corporations are part of various Anglo-Saxon groups, or are shared by the gentiles in general. There are several exceptions, however. One is Ford Motor, which was nurtured to financial maturity by Sidney Weinberg of Goldman, Sachs. It is headed by Democratic fat cat Henry Ford, II ($40,000 to LBJ in 1964, $30,000 to HHH in 1968), who announced in June, 1971, in a not unperceptive jest, that it was necessary to elect a Democratic President in 1972 so he could start living like a Republican again.

Another important exception to the rule is Allied Chemical, a company organized in 1920 by former Lazard Freres partner Eugene Meyer. Allied Chemical still floats its stock through Lazard Freres, which has the assistance of Loeb, Rhoades and Lehman Brothers in this endeavor. The president of the company, it might be noted, is a former Democratic Secretary of Commerce who is a New

Jersey member of the Democrats' National Finance Council.*

American Metal Climax, with partners from Lehman Brothers and Loeb, Rhoades on the board, is also clearly in the big leagues of industrial and mining corporations. (Its dominant figure, Harold K. Hochschild, has usually kept his donations to Democratic presidential candidates in the $20–$30,000 range, and he may have given even more than that to Eugene McCarthy in 1968.) Avco, a semiconglomerate that has grown rapidly under the watchful eye of Lehman Brothers, is now No. 159 on *Fortune's* 500. Avco is also noteworthy because it has perhaps the most "Democratic" management among manufacturing companies within the clique. Whereas most companies have one or two prominent Democrats among their top leadership, Avco had four directors and officers who were Democratic contributors of $500 or more in 1968.

There are some very impressive oil companies (e.g.,

---

* The descendants of Eugene Meyer, who still own a large share of Allied Chemical, are also the owners of one of the publishing empires most abhorrent to Spiro Agnew, the Washington *Post-Newsweek* combine. Interlocking directorships tie Allied Chemical and the Washington Post Company even closer together, and Lazard Freres markets the securities of both companies. Completing the circle, André Meyer of *Lazard Freres* is a relative of the Meyer family that owns the *Post* and *Newsweek*.

Perhaps it is not surprising, then, to learn that the president of *Post-Newsweek*'s radio and television stations is a member of the Democratic Party's National Finance Council, and that Katherine Meyer Graham, chairman of the company, is a regular Democratic contributor. However, it is bemusing, in the light of Agnew's fulminations against the Washington *Post*, to find that Nixon's Secretary of State, William P. Rogers, was a director of the company before joining the cabinet. It also makes the point once again that there are plenty of prominent Republicans from the gentile business community intermingling with members of the Jewish-Cowboy clique.

Amerada-Hess, Tidewater, Kerr-McGee, Halliburton)
within the Jewish-Cowboy orbits. The clique also fares
well in airlines (e.g., American, Braniff, Continental),
even better in movies (e.g., Paramount, Twentieth Cen-
tury-Fox, MGM), and best of all in consumer goods and
merchandising, where Sears, Jewel Tea, Gimbel's, Macy's,
City Stores, Allied Department Stores, Interstate Department Stores, and Federated Department Stores head a
star-studded list.

The assets within the group are rounded out by vast
real-estate holdings, numerous lesser-known corporations
in a variety of light industries, and several of the flashiest
conglomerates—Gulf and Western, LTV, City Investing,
Northwest Industries—of the late sixties.

The Texas anchor of the Jewish-Cowboy clique de-
serves a slightly closer look, for the Texans destined to
raise the biggest money for the national Democratic Party
are, by and large, men who have financial arrangements
with the Jewish bankers on Wall Street. I say "by and
large" because there are certainly big-spending Texas
Democrats—such as those around Continental Oil and the
large cotton firm of Anderson, Clayton—who have their
major dealings with Morgan Guaranty Trust and other
gentile financial institutions. Lloyd Bentsen, the new multimillionaire Democratic Senator from Texas, is not particularly close to any Jewish businessmen either. The
boards from which he resigned to enter politics—Continental Oil, Panhandle Eastern, Trunkline Gas, Bank of
the Southwest, and Lockheed—have few, if any, involve-
ments with the Jewish side of Wall Street. The same is true
for Lincoln Consolidated, the holding company through
which Bentsen manipulates five mutual funds, a $76 mil-
lion insurance company, and six small banks.

But all this is only by way of saying that Texas is a big place and repeating that there are no simple economic and political divisions within the highly integrated corporate community. When we look a little closer, however, in a search for key Democratic fund raisers and fat cats, we find prominent members of the Jewish-Cowboy clique.

We find, for instance, John D. Murchison, who along with his brother manages a billion-dollar empire that includes banking, oil, real estate, construction, and a variety of smaller businesses from air guns to taxicabs. Also in the group is George R. Brown, an important figure in Halliburton Oil; his Brown and Root Construction Company was intimately involved in financing the career of Lyndon B. Johnson. Then there are insurance wheeler-dealers Troy V. Post and Gus Wortham, both of whom are in command of companies all over the country.* All of the above-named kingpins of the mainstream Texas Democrats are involved in one way or another with Lehman Brothers and Goldman, Sachs.

Indeed, it was Lehman Brothers and Goldman, Sachs who helped Texans Troy V. Post and his whiz-kid protégé Jimmy Ling in their takeover bids on old-line Yankee firms. Working through Ling-Temco-Vought, an electronics company established by Ling shortly after World War II, the most sensational play by Post and Ling involved the capture of Wilson and Company in 1967, a maneuver financed in good part by a consortium of six-

---

* Post, for instance, has a twenty-four percent interest in a California insurance company, Legal Reserve Life, where another sizable owner is California oilman and Democratic fat cat Ed Pauley. Post and Pauley also own together a little island off the coast of Hawaii where VIP's often meet for quiet vacations.

teen European banks that Ling had been able to contact
thanks to the intercessions of Lehman partners.*

The Jewish-Cowboy business clique, then, is a formid-
able one. However, it is far from the crème de la crème.
Texas oil men . . . Jewish businessmen . . . smaller companies . . . retailers—this is not the heart of the power
elite. The Jewish-Cowboy group is the major fringe group
in an overwhelmingly Anglo-Saxon power elite rooted in
commercial banking, insurance, public utilities, railroads,
and manufacturing—precisely the areas from which people of Jewish background are almost completely excluded.
Even where the Jews and the Cowboys are highly visible,
as in investment banking, oil, and real estate, they are
decidedly minor leaguers compared to the even wealthier
gentiles.

Texas oil men are super-rich, but even more unbelievably wealthy are the Rockefellers, Mellons, and other
Northerners who own much of the oil business in Texas.
Some Jewish landlords—like Democratic money raiser
Ben Swig in San Francisco, or Democratic fat cat Lawrence Wein in New York—are worth hundreds of millions.
But this is as nothing compared to the true giants of real
estate, who are the same gentile corporation owners who
dominate oil, rails, insurance, utilities, and manufacturing. Through their corporations, the wealthy gentiles are

---

* More than one observer of the Republican onslaught against the
conglomerates in 1969 and 1970 mentioned that the merger kings were
often Jews or Texans. However, few noted that the upstarts usually had
the help of Lehman Brothers, Goldman, Sachs, and Lazard Freres as
their investment bankers. That is, they did not see that the Jewish-Cowboy
clique, through its tremendous influence in Democratic administrations,
had encroached on the turf of the sedate gentiles with overwhelmingly
Republican sensibilities.

the major landowners, the major land developers (by means of real-estate subsidiaries), and the overflowing tenants of large office buildings.

The secondary, dependent nature of the Jewish-Cowboy group is even more apparent in studying the gargantuan commercial banks and insurance companies where both Yankee and Jewish investment bankers obtain much of the long-term capital which they in turn provide to their corporate customers. Although each Jewish investment house has some connections at one or more of these money sources (and Lehman Brothers and Lazard Freres even serve as the investment bankers for Chase Manhattan Bank), it is still the case that not one of the largest commercial banks or insurance companies in New York is part of the Jewish-Cowboy clique. You have to go further down the scale, to Bank of New York–Empire Trust Company (No. 23 among financials), where the families involved in Loeb, Rhoades have a large stock interest, or to CIT Financial Corporation, where Kuhn, Loeb representatives have an important voice, before large lending institutions are to be found that have familial or stock ownership ties to Jewish investment bankers.

JEWS AND DEMOCRATS

The division of Wall Street investment bankers into Yankees and Jews in the early years of American corporate feudalism did not immediately reflect itself in Republican and Democratic allegiances. Although both groups had significant minority representation in the Southern-dominated Democrats, the Jews were as predominantly Republican as their gentile counterparts, whom they resembled in their stiff manners, quiet dignity, and high regard for formal culture.

With the onset of the Depression, however, the polarization of gentiles and Jews began to reflect itself in political affairs. Just why most of the Anglo-Saxon money changers withdrew from the Democrats and the wealthy Jews slowly joined the more recently arrived (and poorer) Eastern European Jews in the Democratic Party is not an easy question to answer—except for those who are sure that one or another grand theory about the nature of man and society is without doubt the correct one. An answer would require the delicate weighing of economic imperatives and cultural values in a way that psychology and sociology are nowhere near achieving.

Some believe the separation came about because the New Deal appealed to Jewish cultural traditions of social justice and charity while at the same time offending the moralistic Protestant belief that people get what they deserve and that poverty is therefore a mark of weakness and sin. Others, such as social critic Ferdinand Lundberg, sociologist E. Digby Baltzell, and one of my informants from a prominent Jewish banking house, suggest that the retail, movie, and consumer-oriented businesses in which many Jewish businessmen made their living made them more sympathetic to the New Deal economic measures designed to increase consumer spending.*

---

* Democrats among Jewish investment bankers are divided in explaining their political preferences. For example, one Wall Street Democrat assured me that Democratic preferences among his business associates were a "spillover" from the general cultural values of the wealthy German-Jewish community in New York; he was highly skeptical of an "economic" explanation in terms of business needs. However, the day after his interview, an even more prominent Democrat on Wall Street stated the

Whatever the reason, Franklin Roosevelt had several very rich Jewish businessmen in his financial inner circle. Heading the list was Herbert Lehman of Lehman Brothers, a Democrat by birth who became governor of New York when Roosevelt moved on to the White House. Another Jewish millionaire of great importance was Henry Morgenthau, Sr., a Lehman in-law with large holdings in Underwood Corporation. His son became Roosevelt's Secretary of the Treasury. Also good for tens of thousands of dollars in contributions to the party were Jesse Straus of Macy's, Howard Cullman of Philip Morris (a Lehman-financed firm), and Bernard Baruch.

The rise of Nazism also helped to move Jewish business leaders along in their transition to the Democratic Party, for FDR was being called "Rosenfelt" by potentially-fascist right-wing Republicans, and many anti-Semitic, racist American gentiles were singing this little ditty about Roosevelt and his wife: "You kiss the niggers and I'll kiss the Jews, and we'll stay in the White House as long as we choose."

Postwar events did nothing to reverse the trend toward the Democrats among wealthy American Jewry. The party, after some slight hesitations, came out in support of the new state of Israel, and in the early fifties the wit and urbanity of patrician Adlai E. Stevenson seemed to attract even more Jews, such as the Meyers of the Washington *Post*, into the arms of the Democrats. The pull of Stevenson, moreover, was combined with an antipathy on the part of many Jews for the antics of Joe McCarthy.

---

economic explanation as if he had read it in Lundberg's *America's Sixty Families*. Interviews did not clear up this question for me.

Barry Goldwater's candidacy in 1964 was perhaps the high point of wealthy Jewish involvement in the Democratic Party, partly because the moderate Republicans from the Jewish finance houses didn't like Goldwater's views and swung to the Democrats, partly because they do the investment banking for the Cowboy multimillionaires of the Southwest who bankrolled Lyndon Johnson.

Some Goldwater defectors, such as John L. Loeb, stayed around to lead the Democratic financial forces in 1968. "I rather enjoyed the political involvement," Loeb told me with a smile. "I still support good Republicans, of course, because I'm more interested in encouraging good candidates than in party, but mostly I support Democrats now." But most moderate Republicans among Jews returned to the Republican fold after the Goldwater debacle.

Yet, even allowing for the swing back to Nixon in 1968 by many anti-Goldwater Republicans, during the sixties the Jewish financial community did become the source of those few Democrats to be found on Wall Street. Moreover, Jewish investment bankers combined with other Jews around the country, many of whom were their customers, to provide the financial leadership of the Democratic Party in every major non-Southern city except Boston, where Irish Catholics grouped around the Kennedys still reign supreme.

In New York, for example, the major Democratic money raisers, in addition to the Jewish investment bankers already mentioned, are Jews Arthur Krim, Robert Benjamin, and Arnold Picker of United Artists. They have plenty of help from a gentile friend, Robert Dowling, who sits on their United Artists board in addition to chairing City Investing, a Lehman-financed real-estate and manu-

facturing conglomerate. But the majority of their big
donors are Jewish.

The leading Democratic fund raiser in Pennsylvania
for many decades was Albert M. Greenfield, whose enterprises encompassed about ten percent of Philadelphia's
business district by the late fifties. Now that he is dead,
the mantle probably will fall to Gustave Amsterdam of
Greenfield's Bankers Securities Corporation, a company
which controls at least five hotels, three department stores,
and three specialty stores. He will have assistance, however, from other prominent Jews such as Frederic Mann,
president of the Industrial Container Corporation, Philip
Berman, president of Hess Department Store, and Aaron
Goldman of Macke Vending Company. (Irishman Matt
McCloskey also will continue as a leading money raiser.)

Out in Chicago, to take one example from the Midwest, the role of Jewish businessmen in party finance can
be seen most quickly in the fact that twenty-nine of the
approximately 120 men who gave $1,000 or more to LBJ's
President's Club in 1964 were members of the highly-ex-
clusive, Jewish-only Standard Club, whereas only ten
could be identified as members of the Chicago Club, the
non-Semitic stronghold of the wealthy gentiles in that
city.

Jumping to the West Coast, the names to reckon with
in San Francisco Democratic financing are real-estate men
Ben Swig and Walter Shorenstein, with more than a little
bit of help from their friend and business associate Adolph
Schuman, president of a dressmaking company. In Los
Angeles, when talk turns to Democratic money, knowledgeable people mention the Hillcrest Group—which
means top money givers like savings-and-loan magnate
Mark Taper, lawyer Eugene Wyman, real-estate develop-

ers Louis and Mark Boyer and Joe Shane, and aluminum manufacturer Lawrence Harvey. The name comes from the fact that they are all members of that city's most exclusive Jewish club, the Hillcrest Country Club.

One large Southern city, New Orleans, finds Jews at the financial helm of the Democrats. This includes first of all the Stern family, which owns a large part of Sears, Roebuck because Mrs. Edith Stern is a daughter of the founder. But it also means investment banker Herman Kohlmeyer of Kohlmeyer & Co., Kohlmeyer attorney Stephen Lemann, and coffee broker Sam Israel, among others.

Even in Texas, where conservative gentile Cowboys dominate the Democratic Party apparatus, the moderate-faced wing has a strong contingent of nationally oriented Jewish financial leaders. Bernard Rapoport, insurance mogul from Waco, is probably the outstanding figure, but lawyer Billy Goldberg of Houston, department-store owner Stanley Marcus, and Raymond Nasher of Dallas are often mentioned in the same breath. Then too, any brief catalog of top-drawer Jewish fund raisers from Texas must include the present treasurer of the Democratic National Committee, Robert Strauss. His Dallas law firm often represents some of the major owners in the Jewish-Cowboy clique.

Study after study suggests how strongly people of Jewish faith identify with the Democratic Party. Despite the prominence of Jewish millionaires as leading party fund raisers in major cities, this Democratic identification is not nearly as strong at the highest social levels of the Jewish community. Within New York's Harmonie Club, the oldest and most exclusive of Jewish men's clubs, as many local members in 1968 gave $500 or more to the Republicans as did to the Democrats. But the thirty-six

Democratic angels did dig a little deeper, giving $155,800 to the Republicans' $138,600. The breakdown was slightly different at the Standard Club, the Harmonie's equivalent in Chicago, where twenty-three resident members gave $43,000 to the Democrats and eleven gave $35,000 to the Republicans.*

Perhaps the best indication of the political inclinations of successful Jewish businessmen can be seen in the recorded donations of the delegates and governors of the American Jewish Committee, the most prestigious Jewish organization in the country. In 1968, forty-three delegates and governors were listed for donations of $161,600 to the Democrats, while twenty-seven gave $91,700 to Republicans. Four gave to both parties, and one even gave $2,000 to George Wallace.**

There are, then, Jewish millionaires in both parties. The wealthiest Jews are not exclusively Democrats. The difference in the two parties is that there are so few Democrats among rich Northern Protestants. This aversion to the Democrats on the part of wealthy gentiles shows up most clearly in the membership lists of the upper crust's exclusive clubs. Thus, 154 members of the California Club in Los Angeles gave to Republicans in 1968, but only five gave to Democrats. The situation was the same for the two other gentile bastions for which we have membership lists, the Pacific Union in San Francisco (eighty-four Re-

---

* In 1965 wealthy Jewish scion R. Peter Straus of the Macy family, a strategist for Robert F. Kennedy, criticized Kennedy in-law Stephen Smith for staying at a club "which is known to discriminate against Jewish people." In 1968, when Smith flew into Chicago to discuss a last-minute draft of Teddy Kennedy, he judiciously set up his headquarters at the Standard Club.
** All analyses of Republican and Democratic donations in this book exclude donations to Republican Senator Jacob Javits of New York, for he regularly attracts donations from fat cats of both parties.

publican angels, five Democratic donors) and the Detroit Club in Detroit (105 Republicans, five Democrats).

More generally, the relative importance of gentiles and Jews in the two parties can be seen in our studies of the fattest of fat cats, donors of $10,000 and more in 1960, 1964, and 1968. There were sixty known Republican contributors of $10,000 or more in 1960—only ten percent of those identifiable as to religion were Jewish. On the other hand, fifty-five percent of all identifiable Democratic donors of $10,000 or more in that year were Jewish. The percentages are similar for 1964—Jewish contributors made up four percent of forty-seven big Republican donors, forty-four percent of sixty-seven Democrat angels.

The picture did not change for the Democrats in 1968. For example, forty-three people lent Humphrey $5.9 million in sums ranging from $5,000 to $250,000. Twenty-two of those forty-three were Jewish, with Jews making up thirteen of the twenty-one who made loans of $100,000 or more. Nor had the patterns altered among the donors of $10,000 and up in 1968, even though the list was greatly lengthened by an extensive effort of the Citizens' Research Foundation. About fourteen percent of the 183 identifiable Republican bigwigs were Jewish; sixty-one percent of the knowables among sixty-four big Democratic donors to Humphrey were Jewish.

A precise determination of the role of Jewish businessmen in financing the Democratic Party is not easily calculated because available information on campaign finance is spotty. Estimates from informants supposedly knowledgeable about the party range from a low of forty percent to a high of sixty-five percent for the total Jewish contribution to non-Southern Democratic candidates for statewide and national offices. Two points seem clear, however. The most prominent fund raisers in many large Northern cities are Jewish. Secondly, Jews, many of whom are business owners or executives within the Jewish-Cowboy clique, form the major contingent among the biggest donors.

GENTILES AND DEMOCRATS

Obviously, not all Democratic financial supporters are Jews or Cowboys. There are also some gentiles mixed in. A handful of these gentiles are Southerners, who are dealt with in the next chapter. Some are well-heeled Catholics, such as the Kennedys and their numerous in-laws, but they are few and far between. As one gentile Wall Street financier of long Democratic experience explained to me after numerous assurances of utter anonymity: "The Jews give to all national candidates, the Protestants give to individual candidates they like, the Italians give locally, and the Irish give not at all." There are persistent rumors that even the Kennedys are not exactly generous with any candidates but their own relatives.

Another contingent of well-to-do gentiles who give money in sums of $500 or more to the Democrats are risen commoners who have climbed the corporate pyramids. Such people are found as presidents and (more frequently) vice-presidents within otherwise solidly Republican citadels. They help provide their companies with "access" to the Democratic Party. That is, they cultivate personal and financial friendships with Democratic politicians so they are assured of a personal and sympathetic hearing for any favor they might want to ask. Thus, vice-chairman Robert B. Stoner of Cummins Engine is an important figure in Democratic finances in Indiana, which balances nicely with the fact that the company's major owner, board chairman J. Irwin Miller, is one of the most prominent Republicans in the country. Examples like the Stoner-Miller combination are numerous.

A notable feature of the risen commoners within corporations is the frequency of their Southern or Catholic origins. This makes them "natural" Democrats who are exceptionally useful in gaining contacts in the halls of Congress. Some such people are hired by the corporations after government service, heightening the suspicion that they are filling the slot of Vice President in Charge of Democratic Affairs within the company.

By far the most significant group of gentiles in Democratic Party financing are those few upper-class Protestants who adhere to the party of the common man. Many of this small handful of patricians are from millionaire families in New York, New Jersey, Pennsylvania, and Delaware—families which have been Democratic since the gradual development of the party in the late 1820's. The Roosevelts and Biddles are the most famous, but Archibald Alexander of New Jersey and Alexis du Pont Bayard of Delaware make the point almost as well. The founding fathers of such families were mercantile and banking capitalists whose fortunes preceded the rise of the larger industrial fortunes. Some were involved in trade with the South.

Other patrician Democrats are from New England mugwump families who abandoned the Republicans in the late nineteenth century. Their history gives some currency to the generalization of Democratic adviser Sydney Hyman that "the Democrats are a large group of second-class roughnecks led nationally by a small group of first-class aristocrats."

The rest of the patrician Democrats are the mellowed scions of wealthy Republican families. There are very few of these defectors, but they have been enormously important to the success of the party. Averell Harriman, son of a predatory empire builder, has been among the most influential Democrats in the nation since the thirties. William McCormick Blair, one of the few Democrats from the Protestant Establishment in Chicago, has played a major supporting role since the fifties.

The Number One Yankee renegade of recent years is John D. Rockefeller, IV, the first of his clan to grace the Democratic rolls. He is on record for a mere $5,000 in 1968, but he started to get into the swing of things by helping Averell Harriman underwrite Edmund Muskie's famous televised rebuttal to Richard Nixon's histrionics on the eve of the 1970 elections. Currently serving as Secretary of State in his adopted state of West Virginia, he may well become President of the United States during the 1980's.

Even where the patrician Democrats can claim long familial allegiance to the party, the stress must be on the paucity of their numbers. Moreover, with rare exceptions, such as former Democratic ambassador Raymond Guest and real-estate developer Roger Stevens, their largesse to the party usually does not transcend the $500 to $5,000 range unless a fellow wealthy or well-born Protestant such as Senator Adlai E. Stevenson, III, of Illinois, Senator John Tunney of California, Senator Claiborne Pell of Rhode Island, or ex-Senator Joseph S. Clark of Pennsylvania is the candidate in question.*

* Most people identify John Tunney only as the son of former heavyweight boxing champion Gene Tunney. John Tunney's mother, however, was a grandniece of Andrew Carnegie, the daughter of a multimillionaire

Wealthy Protestants remain essential beyond their number and contributions because of the respectability and
legitimacy they lend to the party in the eyes of other members of the upper class. Social adjustments do not come
easily to wealthy Republicans, but they seem to tolerate
such changes better when they are brought about under
the guidance of well-bred friends who know how to keep
egalitarian strivings within proper limits.

LAWYERS AND DEMOCRATS

No discussion of the sources of party finance in the
United States would be complete without a consideration of the quiet role of corporation lawyers, for these
legal advisers, who are as much businessmen as lawyers,
are often essential couriers between their corporate clients
and political candidates.

There are three kinds of corporation lawyers—Wall
Street lawyers, Washington lawyers, and local lawyers.
Although their chores overlap, each is to some degree a
specialist in his own type of work.

Wall Street lawyers have the task of translating the
transactions of the investment bankers and commercial
bankers into virtually incomprehensible legalistic language. They are usually upper-class boys or the polished
products of Ivy League schools. They handle the legal
aspects of mergers, prepare prospectuses for security issues, represent clients before governmental agencies

---

yachtsman and steel manufacturer, and a woman of absolutely impeccable
social credentials. Her romance with boxer Tunney, who became a successful businessman in his own right, received considerable attention on
the front pages of *The New York Times* in 1928.

(especially the Securities and Exchange Commission), and serve as members of boards of directors. As alleged generalists who can see the big picture, they often are called upon to serve as government officials in Washington. And some, of course, function as money raisers for the political parties.

Unlike Wall Street lawyers, Washington lawyers are usually liberal-sounding men of middle-class origins who came to Washington with one or another Democratic President and then stayed on after he left to utilize their experience and contacts for the pecuniary benefit of themselves and the fat cats. They use their background with a regulatory agency, executive department, or congressional committee to enable their corporate clients to better circumvent the law and receive special favors. In some cases the smoothest corporate lawyers in Washington are making their fortunes by helping corporate clients wriggle around the very laws they wrote while serving in the government.

Washington lawyers in general play a bigger role as Democratic fund raisers and contributors than do Wall Street lawyers, most of whom tend to be Republicans or small Democratic donors. The Washington lawyers' contacts with corporate rich of both parties can be especially lucrative for the campaign coffers of lesser Senators and Congressmen within the Democratic Party.

Local lawyers, rather obviously, are handymen for the rich man in his home territory. Their chores range from local business problems to political coordinating roles with their kindred in New York and Washington. Some, such as Jerry Cardin in Maryland and Eugene Wyman in Los Angeles, are among the Democratic Party's leading fund raisers.

Although there are Democratic and Republican lawyers, there apparently is no such thing as an exclusively Democratic or Republican law firm. With one or two possible exceptions, law firms have partners on both sides of the political fence. Sometimes the coverage is rather impressive. For instance, a large Los Angeles firm, O'Melveny & Myers, houses John O'Melveny, an intimate of conservative Republican Ronald Reagan; Warren Christopher, an adviser to Democratic Senator John Tunney; and Alyn Kreps, a leading figure in the campaigns of Democratic Senator Allan Cranston and Democratic gubernatorial candidate Jesse Unruh.

The label "Democratic" or "Republican" does not mean that the lawyer will refuse to handle cases for fat cats from the other party. To the contrary, as all my interviews made clear, business comes first, and there are no compunctions about undertaking rather dubious cases for wealthy men of very different political coloration. Clark Clifford, Truman's right-hand man in the forties and a Secretary of Defense for Johnson, was happy to make a million dollars helping the du Ponts steer a special capital-gains law through Congress that saved them tens of millions of dollars in taxes. James Rowe, an old New Dealer, finds it possible to lobby for AT&T; and an even more famous New Dealer, Tommy Corcoran, was said by several informants to be a person who helps a wide variety of clients.

Thus, corporate lawyers help render party identifications meaningless when it comes to the day-to-day business problems of the corporate rich. They readily use their influence in one party to help fat cats of the other party receive tax concessions, subsidies, and special rulings from the government. Indeed, it is their Democratic experience which makes so many Washington lawyers valuable to their Republican clients. Theoretically speaking, it would be hard to overestimate the role of these politically-sophisticated lawyers in any listing of the several means by which the power elite gain legal and financial favors from the government no matter which branch of the One Big Property Party happens to be in charge.

Just as there are few Republican or Democratic law firms, there are few major law firms bound exclusively to one or another business clique. However, there are lawyers within several of these firms who have a coordinating role in both the Jewish-Cowboy business clique and the Democratic Party. They run like red threads through both operations, tying together far-flung strands with their overlapping memberships, interlocking directorships, and behind-the-scenes machinations.

One such person is Edwin Weisl, one of the few Jewish partners in Simpson, Thacher, & Bartlett, a Wall Street law firm that grew to prominence as the legal arm of Lehman Brothers. So close was Weisl's relationship to Lehman Brothers that he actually became a limited partner in the late sixties. Weisl's closest friend in the firm was Robert Lehman; one of his closest friends outside the firm was none other than Lyndon Johnson, for whom Weisl has long served as a personal investment adviser. It was Weisl who introduced Robert Lehman to Johnson and induced him to become a late convert to Democratic causes.

Weisl's business duties within the Jewish-Cowboy clique include directorships at Gulf and Western, Cenco Instruments, and U.S. Vitamin Corporation. His last public political chore was as LBJ's Democratic National Committeeman from New York. He now keeps active as a Democratic fund raiser, as does his son, Edwin Weisl, Jr., a member of the Democratic National Finance Council in Washington, D.C.

Another New York lawyer of considerable repute in Democratic circles is Arnold M. Grant, a fund raiser who also was among the party's most generous contributors during the sixties. An associate of the Beverly Hills law firm directed by Eugene Wyman, the most successful Democratic money raiser in Southern California, he serves as a major link among New York, California, and Texas members of the Jewish-Cowboy clique by virtue of his several corporate directorships.

The single most important lawyer in the Jewish-Cowboy clique for the past twenty-five years has been former Supreme Court Justice Abe Fortas. Beginning as a New Deal lawyer, he came to know the Texas rich through his friendship with Lyndon Johnson. His present circle of friendships and business connections includes partners at Lehman Brothers, Goldman, Sachs, and numerous other companies and firms. Fortas' Washington law firm, Arnold, Fortas, and Porter (now Arnold and Porter), is probably the firm most fully integrated into both the Jewish-Cowboy clique and the Democratic Party.

One of the several questionable instances which led to Fortas' embarrassed resignation from the Supreme Court involved his receipt of $15,000 for nine seminar meetings with a class of only seventeen students at American University in Washington, D.C. The money came from a $30,000 fund collected by his former law partner, liberal Democrat Paul Porter, from five former business associates or clients of Fortas and his law firm. The contributors to the Fortas Fund were Maurice Lazarus, vice-chairman of Federated Department Stores; Gustave Lehmann Levy, a partner in Goldman, Sachs and a director of twenty-three corporations; Troy V. Post, chairman of Great-america Corporation and Braniff Airways; Paul D. Smith, general counsel of Philip Morris; and John L. Loeb, senior partner in Carl M. Loeb, Rhoades and a director of eight corporations.

THE PAYOFF

What do the Democratic fund raisers and fat cats among the Jews and the Cowboys get for their money? First, and most crucially, they play a major role in determining the party's presidential candidate. With the exception of a Teddy Kennedy or a Jay Rockefeller, no Democratic presidential candidate can run the fabulously expensive gauntlet that begins in the primaries unless he is adopted by the fat cats of New York, California, and Texas.

The fat cats are essential because no other group within the Democratic Party is able to raise the necessary funds. The Northern liberals usually don't have the resources to back a presidential campaign as well as they did Eugene McCarthy's in 1968, when $11 million in antiwar money was raised. As for the Southern conservatives, they wouldn't be interested in financing a half-way presentable candidate even if they could. And the trade unions are strictly bit players when it comes to financing presidential politics, especially at the level of primary elections. So a Democratic presidential hopeful must be acceptable to the Jews and the Cowboys or forget about winning; the fat cats can sit on their wallets and live with a Republican presidency if the occasion demands. Indeed, many chose wallet-sitting in 1968.

Democratic fat cats also are necessary adjuncts to candidates for Governor and Senator in the most populous states. As a well-heeled California liberal sadly told me, middle-class and labor money simply cannot compete with the big-money candidates in the large states. "We back liberal Congressmen in races where $25,000 or $30,-000 can make a difference," he sighed. "Or we send a few thousand dollars to liberal Senators in small states where you can run a decent campaign without a million dollars." Friendly relationships with Senators and Governors whom they have helped to elect, in turn, give the checkbook Democrats a great deal of leverage at all levels of a state party.

Wealthy Democrats also have considerable clout in mayoralty races in major cities such as New York, San Francisco, and New Orleans. When multimillionaire Ben Swig, to take the most striking example, brought together eighty-five people in 1967 and collected $203,000 in forty-five minutes for the last-minute mayoralty campaign of Joseph Alioto, the other candidates saw the handwriting on the wall. "You can't be elected dogcatcher here without his blessing," claims one San Francisco observer.

When it comes to big offices, then, heavy money has very good strings on any successful Democratic candidate, which means the oil men will continue to enjoy their depletion allowances, the real-estate operators will retain their lucrative depreciation write-offs, and the regressive tax structure will remain an issue that is rarely discussed no matter which party wins the regular election. The political analysts may be right that the Democratic Party is "fragmented," and that it presents different varieties of platforms and political activists at the local, state, and national levels. But it is also true that the same few wealthy men decide which of the candidates will receive the millions of dollars that are a necessary minimum in major primary and general elections. When all the shouting and posturing has died down and the hard-cash facts begin to emerge, there is a familiarity about the business connections of the fat cats who call the decisive shots.

3

THE SOUTHERN ALBATROSS

"If only we could get rid of those nasty Southerners, then we could bring social and economic justice to all Americans." So runs the familiar lament of the ever-hopeful among Northern Democrats, who seem to view Southern Democrats as unwelcome intruders into their forward-looking party of the common man. But the idealists' emphasis is sadly misplaced—*they* are the interlopers. The Democratic Party was the party of the Southern upper classes long before it was the party of the Northern masses, and even after all the New Deals, Fair Deals, and Civil Rights Acts are duly noted, the party still remains in fundamental respects their special sugar daddy. The party of the common man is freighted with a Southern albatross of no little consequence.

Southern politics is renowned for its strange mixture of Confederate buffoons, racist demagogues, and gracious Kentucky colonels, but when we look behind this colorful facade, we find a group of Democratic fat cats who are remarkably similar to the wealthy men who finance the lackluster Republican Party in the North. Both groups of millionaires are white, Anglo-Saxon, and Episcopalian. Both are alumni of prep schools and members of anti-Semitic, anti-Negro gentlemen's clubs. Their wives are the leaders of the Junior League, their daughters are the future debutantes. Further, fat-cat Democrats in the South and the financial angels of the Republicans in the North are the leading bankers, lawyers, and businessmen of their regions, sharing similar views on most—but not all—economic and political matters.

Southern Democratic moneymen, then, are more like Republicans in very thin disguise. "Oh, our business community is solidly Democratic in its registration," explained one South Carolinian, "but their hearts are with the Northern Republicans." "There's a group of fifteen to twenty big businessmen who get together to back local Democratic candidates," said an expert on New Orleans politics, "but I'd guess a majority of them are national Republicans in their sympathies." Only occasionally would an informant suddenly change his tone and say of a Southern fat cat, "Now he's a real, honest-to-god national Democrat," by which is meant someone who does not twitch when a friendly remark is dropped about labor unions, blacks, or the Social Security program.

Everywhere in the South the story was essentially the same—the upper classes rule the party's finances—so I will mention only the most prominent examples. In Virginia, the owners of Reynolds Metals assume a pivotal role in campaign finance, with board chairman Richard S. Reynolds, Jr., serving in recent years as state party chairman. What makes the Reynolds family unusual among Southern donors is that they have been contributing sizable amounts to Democratic presidential campaigns since 1936. Their high-water mark was 1956, when three Reynolds brothers are on record for $18,000 to Adlai Stevenson and their tobacco-rich cousins in North Carolina chipped in with at least another $24,000.

In Georgia, two or three major business empires dominate the financing of politics. Towering above all the rest are the owners and directors of Atlanta-based Coca-Cola, one of the nation's largest and most international corporations. The company is the center of a business complex that also includes leading Georgia banks and several minor companies. Right behind the Coke people in stature is Mills B. Lane, Jr., chairman of Citizens and Southern Bank, one of the South's two or three largest banks. The jovial Lane is considered one of the few national Democrats among Southern money raisers.

Louisiana fat cats have formed themselves into a group called the Cold Water Committee, for the purpose of backing mildly progressive Democratic candidates. Among the members are several multimillionaires connected with the Whitney National Bank, the largest bank in the region. At the core of the group is a clique some critics like to call the Stern Group, which is anchored in the Sears, Roebuck fortune of Mrs. Edith Rosenwald Stern and the New Orleans investment banking firm of Kohlmeyer & Co. The Stern Group has fraternal and business relations with New York Democrats and New York investment bankers within the Jewish-Cowboy interest group.*

Among checkbook Democrats in Louisiana not on the Cold Water Committee is the largest individual stockholder in the Whitney National Bank, Walter G. Helis, Jr., an oil multimillionaire of Greek extraction who is a personal friend of Spiro T. Agnew. Helis is down for $15,000 to LBJ in 1964 and $20,000 to Humphrey in 1968. Locally, he is rumored to have spent $150,000 on a mayoralty candidate.

Arkansas is one of the poorest states in the Union, but it has several citizens worth tens of millions who are loyal Democrats. C. H. Murphy, Jr., chairman of the Democratic National Finance Council for the state, is a major owner of Murphy Oil Company (total assets—$286.4 million). Witt Stephens, another big contributor, controls Arkansas-Louisiana Gas Company, a natural-gas

---

* The Stern Group may be in the process of performing an important service for the nation's entire power elite. They are contesting in court the traditional Internal Revenue Service ruling that large political donations such as those given by the Sterns are subject to federal gift taxes ranging from two and a quarter percent on anything over $3,000 per candidate to as high as fifty-seven percent on larger sums.

In 1969 Mrs. Stern, with the aid of investment banker Herman Kohlmeyer, contractor Gervais Favrot, lawyer Thomas Lemann, and her son, Edgar B. Stern, Jr., filed a suit in the local district court charging that the $60,000 she spent in two state political contests should not be subject to $28,000 in gift taxes. This was on the rationale that the money was in fact a business expenditure "motivated by a desire to protect her property and personal interests." The gift tax did not apply, she claimed, because her largesses was not prompted by "affection, respect, admiration, charity, or like impulses."

The judge agreed with her, and so did the U.S. Court of Appeals for the Fifth Circuit, to which the Internal Revenue Service appealed the case. The question may end up in the Supreme Court. The fat cats would probably settle for removal of the gift tax on large donations, but if they get everything they want, they will actually be able to deduct their large donations from their income taxes as a business expense.

producer in eastern Arkansas and northern Louisiana (total assets—$427.3 million). As for Ray Rebsamen, who sits on the board of Witt Stephens' natural-gas company, he may be worth $100 million thanks to banks, insurance companies, and auto dealerships. There are other fat cats in Arkansas, but they hardly seem worth mentioning in the same breath with the fortunes of Murphy, Stephens, and Rebsamen.*

The involvement of the most substantial business interests in the South with the Democratic Party also appears in the corporate connections of several prominent Senators. Senator B. Everett Jordan of North Carolina, for example, whose family controls Jordan Spinning Mills, Royal Cotton Mills, and Seller Manufacturing Company, until recently sat on the board of directors of Winston-Salem's Wachovia Bank & Trust, the largest bank in the South, despite his many duties in Washington. At board meetings he met with presidents and directors from such pillars of the North Carolina business world as Hanes Knitting, R. J. Reynolds Tobacco, Burlington Industries, Jefferson Standard Life Insurance, and Belk Department Stores. However, Jordan is only one of the reasons why everyone agrees that North Carolina has a no-nonsense, respectably conservative Democratic government that is completely dominated by millionaire businessmen.

As for Arkansas' senior Senator, John McClellan, chairman of the Senate Committee on Government Operations,

---

* C. H. Murphy, Jr. is seldom recorded as giving more than $5,000 to a political candidate. When I mentioned that figure to an intimate of Arkansas politics, he scoffed and estimated that Murphy probably gives at least $50,000 to any candidate in whom he is interested. This informant once was handed an envelope with $5,000 in cash by one of Murphy's associates.

he sits on the board of the First National Bank of Little
Rock, one of the biggest banks in the state. "It's a gross
conflict of interest," exclaimed one Arkansas newsman.
"There have been several editorials criticizing his decision
to stay on that board, but they don't seem to bother him."
The late Drew Pearson claimed McClellan is widely
hailed as the "banking industry's most obedient champion
in the Senate."

Then too, McClellan's law firm represents several of the
leading companies in the state, including Arkansas Power
and Light, a corporation headed for many years by a Mc-
Clellan law partner. In addition to all this, McClellan
owns a large share of Midwest Video, a TV chain with
operations in Mississippi, Texas, and New Mexico as well
as Arkansas. In 1957 the company joined forces with
KTBC-TV of Austin, Texas, which is owned by Lyndon
and Lady Bird Johnson.

But enough is enough—there is no need to dwell on the
details of the oil millions of Louisiana Senator Russell
Long, the life-insurance company of Georgia Senator Eugene Talmadge, or the numerous business enterprises of
Arkansas Senator William Fulbright. It should be apparent by now that the heftiest of the fat cats in the South,
as well as many of their smoothest politicians, are business
magnates who have much in common with Northern Republicans.

The only other outcome of our investigation of Southern
fund raisers worth note here is the intimate linkage between Southern Democrats and Northern Republicans in
the ownership, financing, and management of many of
the largest companies in the South. These connections
date back to the post-Civil War era when Morgans,
Rockefellers, Mellons, and other super-rich Northern fami-

lies converted the South, often with the connivance of leading Southerners of that period, into an economic colony of the North. Thus, the railroads and utilities so well-known for dominating Southern state legislatures are in good part directed from Wall Street in New York and State Street in Boston. Mississippi Democrat LeRoy Percy, a multimillionaire with cotton, fertilizer, and banking interests, sits on the board of Middle South Utilities, the holding company that controls power companies in Mississippi, Arkansas, and Louisiana. But so do upright Northern Republicans like Pericles Stathas of Chicago, who is on the boards of numerous gas, oil, and electric companies. The president of Southern Railways, W. G. Claytor, Jr., is a Southern Democrat who gave $1,000 to Humphrey in 1968, but his board includes such Northern Republicans as Jeremiah Milbank, a Nixon finance chairman who contributed at least $11,500 to the Republicans in 1968. (Which is only a little less than the $20,000 he and his family gave to Republican causes in 1964.)

The Northern influence in Alabama and South Carolina is more blatant than in any other part of the South. "The capital of Alabama is really in Pittsburgh and New York," said one lawyer familiar with the state. He was primarily referring to the fact that the big iron and steel works of Alabama are owned by Northerners, especially the Northerners who control U.S. Steel.

Over in South Carolina, seventy percent of the labor force is employed in textile mills that are predominantly owned outside the state. As in the case of the major railroad companies, the leading aerospace companies, and the largest utilities, the Northern connections of these textile firms are almost exclusively with top-drawer gentile banks in New York, banks such as Morgan Guaranty Trust and

First National City Bank. One has to look far and wide to
find a major Southern corporation with ties to the German-Jewish investment bankers so essential to Northern
Democrats.

WHY AREN'T THE SOUTHERN RICH REPUBLICAN?

If Northern and Southern gentiles of great wealth have
so much in common, and share so many business connections, why is one group Republican and the other Democratic? The obvious answer seems to lie in the Civil War
and Reconstruction, but there is more to it than that. Indeed, a close reading of post-Reconstruction history reveals extreme Republican sympathies on the part of the
upper class in the South. The motives behind their ultimate rejection of explicit Republican self-identification
may explain the weaknesses of recent GOP attempts to
convert the higher levels of Southern society to the Republican banner. It turns out that a Southern Strategy
has been tried before with as little success as the Nixon
attempt of 1970.

Lest anyone has forgotten, and it is amazing how many
Southerners have *not* forgotten, the Republicans rose to
power as an antislavery party. It was the Republicans,
not the Democrats, who harbored a militant abolitionist
wing, a fact which was turning wealthy Southern Whigs
toward the Democrats throughout the 1850's. While the
Civil War certainly did nothing to endear Republicans to
Southerners, there were in 1865 some influential Southerners who hoped for benign terms from the GOP and
eventual rapprochement with that party. Reconstruction,
the program of the Radical Republicans that was under-
taken in 1866, ended all such dreams.

Given the bitter myths many Southerners perpetuate about the Civil War and Reconstruction, the question of Southern adherence to the Democratic Party seems to have found a simple answer. As already suggested, however, there is more to the problem than immediately meets the eye. It seems that in 1877 the Northern Republicans entered into a complex bargain with the Southerners which was supposed to lead, among other things, to the eventual movement of the Southern upper class to the Republican Party.

There were several background factors growing out of the Reconstruction period which set the stage for the Compromise of 1877. For one thing, the defeated Southerners used every possible means, including violence, to resist Reconstruction successfully and put the Negro back on the bottom of society. At the same time, Northern support for the Republican policy of military occupation and government by blacks and carpetbaggers had gradually waned—partly because most Northerners didn't have any more respect or concern for Negroes than Southerners did, partly because Northern businessmen wanted stable Southern governments run by conservative whites.

The result of these and other pressures was the gradual erosion of the Republican policy in the South. By 1874 the Democrats were in control in the House of Representatives and in all but four of the old Confederate States. Many cautious Republicans began calling for rapprochement with Southern "redeemers" who had agreed to accept the business-oriented measures enacted by the Yankee capitalists while the Southern planters were out of the Union.

A crisis that made a semiformal compromise necessary occurred in 1876 when there was a dispute over whether

the Democrat Samuel Tilden or the Republican Ruther-
ford Hayes had captured the presidency. Tilden had
clearly won 184 electoral votes, only one short of a majority, but the Republicans disputed his seeming victories
in Louisiana, South Carolina, and Florida, any one of
which would have given him a majority in the electoral
college. On the other hand, if all the disputed votes were
given to Hayes by the carpetbagger regimes in the disputed states, he would win the presidency by one electoral vote. So the argument began as to who should certify
the vote in each of the three states.

While all of the shouting and threatening was going on,
top-brass Southerners quietly told influential Republicans
that they didn't want trouble or violence. Nor did Northern big businessmen, who by then had made large investments in the South and had entered into a variety of
business relationships with many of the defeated Southerners. Furthermore, 1876 had been the worst year of a
three-year depression, and there was labor unrest in the
East and agrarian discontent in the West. Clearly, it was
a time for men of property to put aside minor squabbles.

The stage was thus set for negotiations between friends
of Hayes and Southern spokesmen from the border states
of Kentucky and Tennessee. There followed months of
complicated maneuvering by agents on both sides, which
finally boiled down to a delicate compromise: The Republicans were to occupy the presidency, which was the
biggest prize of all, while the Southerners were to have
all occupation troops removed from the South, the assur-
ance of the appointment of Southern Democrats to key
posts in the South, and Republican support of subsidies
for railroad construction, levee reconstruction, and other
expensive building projects greatly desired by the Southern gentry.

While the presidency, troop removal, Southern appoint-
ments, and subsidies were the most essential ingredients
in the bargain, there was another consideration, at least
on the part of leading Republicans. They wanted to convert their Southern friends into Republicans. Having had
enough of black allies in the South, they wanted the
Southern branch of the Republican party to be managed
by businessmen of conservative economic tastes. They
sought stalwarts, wrote historian C. Vann Woodward,
who had been Whigs before the Civil War: "An old Whig,
like many Southern leaders who now called themselves
Democrats or conservatives, Hayes dreamed of breaking
down the sectional barrier between men of property and
reviving the ante-bellum political alliance between conservatives of North and South." As Hayes' Secretary of
the Treasury put it: "What we wish is to combine, if possible, in harmonious political action the same class of men
in the South as are Republicans, that is the producing
classes, men who are interested in industry and property."

On the other side of the fence, many wealthy Southerners encouraged Hayes and the Republicans in their
hopes. Some Southerners said the subsidies would do
the trick, particularly because Northern Democrats in
Congress had not been very supportive of such measures
for the South. Others claimed the appointment of sound
Southern Democrats to influential posts would trigger the
conversion process.

Why did the plan to make wealthy Southern Democrats into Republicans fail? While there were some break-
downs in the bargain of 1877 that may have played a
part, and some Radical Republicans continued to rail
against Southern Democrats, the big factor seems to have
been the unrest that continued to develop in the under

classes in the South. As the Southern rich began to have more and more trouble at home with poor whites who wanted to make common cause with Western agrarians, they came to fear the abandonment of the Democratic Party to the underprivileged. They realized the two-party system would open up political competition and bring Negroes into the equation as the balance of power. There was only one thing to do in order to protect their economic privileges—stay in the Democratic Party and make racial slurs about anyone who tried to bring about better wages for workers or a better shake for small farmers through the Republican Party or a third party. As part of this strategy to keep the white masses in line, the Democratic Party was locally sold as the white man's party and the Republicans were excoriated as the vicious perpetrators of Civil War and Reconstruction.

The collapse of the Republicans' Southern Strategy, then, came about not primarily because of disagreements between Northerners and Southerners of property and substance, but because of the problems the Southerners faced in their own region. The one-party system that had developed in the South was an ideal device for a struggling Southern ruling class that had to extract every extra ounce of sweat out of its workers and tenant farmers if it was going to live well and pay tribute to Yankee financiers at the same time. The Southern Democratic rich thus became junior partners to the Northern Republican multimillionaires at the expense of other, racially divided socioeconomic classes in their region. They thereby helped mark the South as a region of extremely low wages, highly regressive taxes, and minimal expenditures for schools and public services.

The under-dogs did not take this treatment passively,

at least not for the first twenty or thirty years. Some impoverished agrarians tried working with the Republicans, but conservative Northern Republicans wanted no part of a political alliance with riffraff. Others organized cooperatives and boycotted the overpriced merchandise of the big businesses, but they were denounced as socialists, roughed up, and even killed by wealthy Southerners and their agents.

In the 1890's, when the farmers organized their own Populist Party and made tentative overtures to blacks, the rulers were clearly on the defensive. They countered with sugar-coated Democratic platforms, hysterical race-baiting, and more violence. The major outcome of this upsurge, from the point of view of those at the bottom, was the disenfranchisement of all blacks and many poor whites. After that there was no serious challenge to the Southern oligarchy for more than sixty years. The question of Republican allegiance became academic.

THE SOUTHERN STRATEGY TODAY

Ever since the Southern upper crust entered into its deal with the Northern Republicans in 1877, the break-up of the solid South has been considered imminent by the acknowledged experts of the day. During the first fifty to sixty years of the New South, it was the growth of industrialization that was supposed to be leading to this change. After World War II this argument was supplemented by the decline in the percentage of blacks in the Southern population and the increase in Republican presidential voting in urban middle-class areas. In the sixties the securing of the right to vote by blacks was added as yet another factor working against one-party politics.

But it is not going to happen. Contrary to all economic and philosophic rationale, the Southern Democrats are not about to become Republicans despite the theoretical justifications advanced by political scientists and the heavy-handed demagoguery of Richard Nixon and Spiro Agnew. For what is overlooked in all the statistics is the absence of avowed Republicans among those who happen to count the most—the closely knit power elite of the Southern states. They may vote Republican nationally, or even give $1,000 or $2,000 to an Eisenhower or a Nixon, but they will continue to consider themselves Democrats and work to control the Democratic Party in their home localities. There are many good reasons for their Democratic fixation, some of which were not obvious to me until I realized I had to explain the absence of a political transition that was supposed to happen but didn't. Before reciting those reasons, it is necessary to establish the facts of the matter.

One of the questions I asked journalists, lawyers, and academicians all over the South was, Are there important businessmen in your state who are backing Republicans? With the exception of two or three states, the uniform answer was that only a few wealthy men are trying to build a Republican Party that could take control of the local courthouse, the state legislature, and Congress. Moreover, those few hardly represent the heart of the business establishment in the various states.

"Most big businessmen in Alabama have been Republican-oriented for a long time," says one of the state's leading journalists, "but they will remain Democrats at the state level. There are only one or two Republicans in the state legislature and the Republicans may even lose their House seats in the '72 election." Similar conclusions were stated by observers in North Carolina, South Carolina, Georgia, and Louisiana.

A seeming exception might appear to be South Carolina, where the biggest fortune in the state has been active in advancing the ultra-right careers of Republicans Barry Goldwater and Strom Thurmond. However, this rich primitive, Roger Milliken, owner of the Deering-Milliken textile empire, is a displaced Rhode Island Yankee who has not been joined in his highly reactionary endeavors by the rest of the South Carolina business community.

Back in the forties a knowledgeable South Carolinian explained to inquiring political scientists that "no matter what is said [about the possibility of becoming Republicans], no person who makes more than $20,000 a year wants a two-party system in South Carolina. . . . With the present Democratic structure, the $20,000-a-year man can keep control of the situation." The continuing truth of those words was evidenced once again in 1970 when the majority of the corporate rich of South Carolina quietly lined up behind Democratic gubernatorial candidate John West against Milliken's racist candidate, Albert Watson, a former Democratic Congressman. West won handily.

Arkansas provides another case where a wealthy Northern Republican was not able to make Republicans out of the native plutocrats. In fact, Arkansas is all the more striking because Winthrop Rockefeller was even richer than Milliken. Furthermore, he was a more modern Republican. And most decisive of all, he was a proved vote getter who had won the Arkansas governorship two straight times. Nevertheless, by all accounts the Arkansas fat cats were very pleased when they were able to beat him in 1970 with a progressive-sounding Democrat

named Dale Bumpers. And as of 1971 there were only
four Republicans in the state legislature—three in the
House and one in the Senate. Despite the many years
of hard work by Rockefeller, there is no future for the
Southern Strategy in Arkansas.

Even in Godforsaken Mississippi, where the last two
presidential votes have gone to the likes of Goldwater and
Wallace, there is little or no movement on the part of the
indigenous rich (such as they are) to the Republicans. "I
hear lots of your people are going Republican," I said to
one Mississippi lawyer with good connections to the respectable moneymen of the national party. "That's pure
bullshit," he drawled as only a Mississippian can drawl,
and then went on to explain that Mississippi, which is
unbelievably poor even by Southern standards, was too
dependent upon government spending and agricultural
subsidies for the local bankers and plantation owners to
defect to a party that likes to cut the federal budget: "I'd
like to have my pockets lined with money while I'm having this race thing stuffed down my throat. We love that
federal money, and Nixon is not delivering the goodies
into Mississippi."

It even turns out that the little Mississippi oligarchy
has a few moderates who gently pushed for a reasonable
governor—a governor likely to comply with national party
guidelines concerning the selection and composition of
the delegation to the 1972 presidential nomination convention. Plantation owner-banker LeRoy Percy was one;
Owen Cooper, who sits on the boards of the Mississippi
Chemical Company and the First Mississippi Corporation
with Percy, was another. D. A. Biglane, whose oil wells
in Natchez are worth a pretty penny, also would like to see
a less raucous Democratic government. So would James

Child, the local lawyer for Illinois Central, a Harriman-controlled company which has more miles of track in Mississippi than it does in Illinois.

The ties of the Mississippi business community to oily Texas Democrats also may serve as a brake on any Republican-leaning tendencies. Lamar Life, the largest life insurance company in Mississippi, is controlled by the Murchisons, who also own a television station in the state capital. Lamar Life, in turn, is close to First National Bank of Jackson, one of the state's two large banks.

There are two or three states where the Southern Strategy may work. Virginia is one; Tennessee, where the Republicans had a base of traditional Republican followers in the mountain country of eastern Tennessee, is another. Nor are Republicans unknown in border states such as Kentucky and Oklahoma. But the basic point remains—the Southern high and mighty are not going to lead a wholesale defection to the Republican Party.

The reasons for the allegiance of the Southern well-to-do to the Democratic Party are complex and intertwined. Some are pragmatic and economic in their basis, others are emotional and psychological. These various reasons are not easily weighed as to their relative importance, nor are they easily separated one from the other, but they can be broken down into four main components.

1. Thanks to the time-honored practice of determining the chairmanships of congressional committees by means of seniority, and since Southern Congressmen are more likely to remain long in office without serious challenge, the one-party system has great value in giving extra leverage in Congress to a region which needs every bit extra it can get. As the Southerners well know, they wouldn't control half the committees of Congress with

their less than one fourth of its membership if they became Republicans. "There is no doubt," wrote one political scientist, "but that the one-party system enables the South to exert more influence in Congress than it could by any other means." The remark was written in 1942 when Southerners dominated the key committees of Rules, Ways and Means, Agriculture, and Banking in the House, and Agriculture, Appropriations, and Finance in the Senate—among others. In 1969, when the Southerners were supposed to be fading in the aftermath of the civil-rights sixties, they were in the saddle as never before, with dominion over ten standing committees in the Senate and seven in the House.*

To become Republicans, then, would cost the Southerners power rather than gain it for them. Unless Dixie fat cats are forced out of their party by Northern liberals, or voted out of control of state party organizations by Southern under classes, they are better off where they are now.

2. The Southern money lords will stay in the Democratic Party because their needs are not completely in harmony with those of their Northern counterparts. I have thus far emphasized the similarities between Northern Republicans and Southern Democrats, but there are also some differences. They agree on most economic and political issues, but that doesn't mean they agree on all of them.

---

* Seniority has been the tradition of the House for sixty years. In the Senate the practice is over a hundred years old, and it had the same effects then as it has now: "In 1859 a Northern Democrat called the seniority usage 'intolerably bad' and complained that it 'has operated to give to Senators from slaveholding states the chairmanship of every single committee that controls the public business of this Government.' "

Studies of voting patterns in Congress suggest that the major differences between Northern Republicans and Southern Democrats arise over federal subsidies. The South, a mismanaged and traditionally agricultural region, needs help if it is to avoid even worse living standards than it now endures. Among the most critical of these subsidies are the handouts to millionaire plantation owners who grow cotton, tobacco, rice, peanuts, and sugar in the rural regions of the Deep South. In 1966, for instance, $985.6 million flowed into eight former Confederate states (including Texas) in agricultural subsidies. About thirteen percent of that went to just 3,097 plantations. A few large landowners received several hundred thousand free dollars.

Ed Mauldin, the biggest cotton grower in Alabama, was on the dole for $101,000 in subsidy payments in that year. It is not likely that his position as Alabama coordinator for Humphrey-Muskie was the consequence of a mere whim. He knows only Democrats, not penny-pinching Republicans, make such gifts possible. But the most celebrated case of all, of course, is Mississippi Senator James Eastland, who is awarded more than $100,000 each year for not growing cotton (e.g., $129,000 in 1966, $160,000 in 1967).

Southern Democrats like subsidies because they cost the South nothing and benefit the rich more than they help the poor. Wealth, these wily fellows have discovered, comes not only from owning the means of production, but from controlling the purse strings of the federal government. They have learned to use the government—through such congressional sinkholes as committees and subcommittees for Agriculture, Public Works, and Military Appropriations—as an agency to take money from

the wage earners of the North and West and funnel it
into the hands of the leisure class in the South. Which is
only poetic justice, they would argue. After all, Yankees
destroyed the slave-based Southern way of life and
turned the area into an economic colony.*

When it comes to legislation that might cost the wealthy
a little money, however, the Southern Democrat suddenly
changes his tune. He becomes an adamant defender of
free enterprise, a vigilante against creeping socialism and
the demoralizing effects of free handouts to the poor.
Translated into dollars and cents, this means he votes
with Northern Republicans to gut any legislation supporting labor unions, minimum wages, or social welfare. Even
when he feels compelled to show loyalty to Northern
Democrats on a labor issue, he first of all extracts concessions which exempt agricultural labor and seasonal workers in cotton and tobacco processing from the protective
provisions of the act, thereby leaving a large contingent
of Southern workers in a state of super-exploitation at the
hands of Southern fat cats.

3. To leave the Democratic Party to blacks, poor
whites, and trade unionists in a region with only a small
middle class would be contrary to self-serving rationality,
especially at a time when blacks strongly identified with
the national Democratic Party are voting in increasing
numbers. "The gut issue of the seventies in the South will
be economic self-interest, not race," predicts a North Carolina journalist familiar with the entire South. "Therefore
a Southern swing to the Republicans is not in the cards

---

* The czars of money in Congress are the chairmen of subcommittees of
the House Committee on Appropriations. In 1971, eight of the twelve
subcommittees were headed by Southerners.

because most people down here are poor." "People in Mississippi are conservative on one issue, race," says an informant there. "Populism lurks in the background on other issues."

In other words, it would be somewhat risky to abandon to more liberal leadership a population identified with the Democrats through mythic traditions and economic interest. If the Southern power elite are to retain their privileges, they must maintain a strong position within the party that has the potential to turn in a more humane direction. Even as things stand now, there are more economic liberals elected in the Solid South than meet the Northern eye.

4. Finally, two psychological traits of the Southern rich, paternalism and fierce regional pride, also help to keep most of them in the Democratic fold. Due to the ideology and psychology bequeathed from the slaveholding past, Southern millionaires tend to be exceptionally paternalistic—in a condescending, self-serving way—in their relationships to underlings, especially black underlings. Thus, Southern gentlemen are not likely to reject a party merely because they have to share it with blacks and poor whites. If anything, they may feel such a party needs their special "leadership" qualities.

The fierce sectional loyalty of the Southerner needs no documentation. Northerners are still "Yankees," Dixie is still the national anthem. Southern identifications are often as important as American ones, and one such important identification is with the South's own political party —the Democrats. Despite the liberal image of the party in the sixties, and the influx of black supporters, it is still *their* party in the minds of many Southerners. "I didn't leave the party, it left me," lament conservative South-

erners, but it is usually said with the pride of possession
which suggests they will continue to try to return it to its
lash-and-chain mentality. In the minds of many Southerners, including the many Dixie aristocrats with deep roots
in the past, the Democrats will be their party for a long
time to come—even if they have to vote Republican every
once in a while in presidential elections in order to keep
the Northern Democrats from besmirching its true principles.

Nixon and Agnew to the contrary, then, the present political arrangements in the South, however confusing they
may be to purists who would like the parties reorganized
along ideological lines, are much more beneficial to Southern wealth holders than would be a formal realignment
with their Northern Republican counterparts. The way
things are now, the Southerners can have their cake and
eat it too. The real Southern Strategy will continue to be
the one developed by Southern leaders a long time ago:
Vote Republican on the presidential level when necessary,
and enter into deals with congressional Republicans to
scuttle labor and welfare legislation, but stay in control
of state and local Democratic organizations so you can
get more out of the federal government and keep a better
hold on the under classes at home.

But it is not only the Southerners who should be happy
with the present state of affairs. The arrangement is
healthy for the nation's super-rich in general, for it helps
maintain a conservative big-business viewpoint in both
political parties. "The Southerners have to stay Democratic so that politics don't polarize around issues," a
Republican political scientist told me. No doubt he was
raised on the words of one of those dangerous Eastern
Establishment Republicans, Thomas Dewey, who noted
in a 1950 lecture at Princeton that a neat little realign-

ment of the two parties along liberal-conservative lines
was not a good idea. It would lead, he warned, to a situation in which "The results would be neatly arranged, too.
The Republicans would lose every election and the Democrats would win every election."

It looks as though the Northern Democrats—even
though they proved unreliable on the race issue—will
have their Southern albatross for a long time to come.

THE MACHINE DEMOCRATS

Thanks to the Democrats, Southern conservatives dominate the all-powerful congressional committees which
make or break progressive legislation of value to the common man. There is, however, nothing sacred about the
seniority system which bestows this power upon them. It
is merely a tradition within the Democratic caucuses that
meet at the beginning of each Congress to select congressional leaders and ritually endorse the committee chairmen offered to them by the seniority system. Moreover,
the Southern ascendancy could not be perpetuated without the help of at least some Northern Democrats, for
Southerners are in the minority among Democrats in both
houses.

In the House of Representatives, for example, there are
about one hundred Southern and border-state Congressmen, and one hundred fifty Northern and Western Congressmen. The one hundred fifty Northerners could make
any one of several possible changes which would loosen
the grip of the Southerners appreciably. It thus becomes
of interest to ask why the Northern Democrats do not push
aside the Southerners and get about the business of ful-
filling some of their campaign promises.

To ask such a question, particularly in the House of

Representatives, confronts us with the amazing specimens who aid and abet the Southerners—the machine Democrats sent to Congress by the political bosses of large Northern cities. Like the Southerners, these machine Democrats are the overaged products of one-party districts. Like the Southerners, they are primarily interested in subsidies, contracts, and handouts for their friends, and often have contempt for their black and poor-white constituents. One former Democratic Congressman told me many of them fear the political potential of the black voters even more than the Southerners do.

Unlike the Southerners, however, the machine Democrats are not the creatures of the most important business interests in their region. They are instead ethnic Americans who look out for the interests of Irish, Italian, Jewish, and Polish businessmen in little uptown banks, construction companies, insurance agencies, real-estate firms, and marginal businesses that sell supplies and services to governmental agencies and large corporations.

Making up about one fourth to one third of the Democratic contingent in the House, these political zombies are often overlooked in all the righteous clamor about Southern domination. It is not noticed that they hold the balance of power between Northern liberals and Southern conservatives, and that more often than not they vote with the Southerners on crucial questions such as party leadership, the seniority system, and the general organization of the House. By siding with the Southerners on these all-important procedural questions, they help set up a system that makes it all but impossible for even mildly reformist legislation to survive. It is a system that encourages delays and back-room deals which can cut the heart out of civil-rights legislation, labor legislation, and welfare appropriations—precisely those measures most needed by the Democratic voters of Northern cities.

Should any mangled progressive legislation manage to make it to the floor of the House, though, the machine Democrats dutifully vote for it, thereby preserving their liberal images for their labor and ethnic constituencies. In short, like the Southerners, the Northern machine Democrats have found a way to have their cake and eat it too. A Washington correspondent for the *Wall Street Journal* put it this way:

> The organization Democrats have largely escaped notice because, until recently, liberal opinion judged Congressmen only by their voting records. On this score, most of the organization men were in an unassailable position; year after year they won liberal ratings of up to 100 per cent from Americans for Democratic Action. Yet in terms of "democratic action," they produced little or nothing. By voting right, they satisfied liberal opinion at home; by doing nothing effective, they satisfied their Southern allies in the House.

What is the basis for this remarkable bargain at the expense of the urban masses? There are those who would explain it in terms of the similarity in the political backgrounds of the Southerners and the machine Democrats. The idea here is that the Irish-run political machine and the Southern courthouse gang both produce nonideological organization men unconcerned with issues, men willing to compromise in order to do favors for their districts. "The House," says the *Wall Street Journal* reporter already quoted, "resembles nothing so much as the city

machine that sent the urban Democrat to Washington."
As wheeler-dealers looking for sure bargains, this line of
argument continues, the machine Democrats prefer the
certainty of an alliance with their Southern colleagues to
a more unsure arrangement with the one hundred or so
Northern Democrats whose districts have been Democratic only since the New Deal and are sometimes recap-
tured by Republicans under unusual circumstances.

But there is probably more to the alliance than these
arguments suggest. The urban Democrat and the Southern Democrat, as already noted, have a very strong financial interest in common—government spending in the
form of subsidies and large federal budgets. Neither could
get what he wants by turning to the tight-fisted Republicans. The trade-off is straightforward—machine Democrats support agricultural subsidies, which are of little
interest to the voters of their districts; Southern Democrats support some housing subsidies and other expenditures of interest to Northern Democrats. The petty rich of
the North and South who are the backers of congressional
Democrats thus join forces against the big-rich Republicans. Unfortunately they do so at the expense of blacks
and organized labor.

There is, then, a wholly sensible pecuniary reason for
machine Democrats trying to keep the Southerners within
the Democratic Party. It allows the party to organize
Congress and keep the gravy flowing. The Southerners
exact a high price—a majority of committee chairmanships through the device of the seniority system, and the
right to side with Northern Republicans against labor and
welfare legislation. But the machine Democrats apparently reason that half a loaf and some committee chairmanships are better than nothing.

As vital as the control of Congress may be to favor seekers, it is not merely in Congressional politics that the Southern Democrats are of great concern to many Northern Democrats. Strange as it may sound, they are also essential in presidential politics, for their conservative state delegations to the national conventions join with the machine Democrats to preclude the nomination of overly liberal candidates for President and Vice-President. In 1944, for example, it was Southern Democrats, goaded by California oil man Ed Pauley and Washington corporation lawyer George E. Allen, who joined with machine Democrats in the North in kicking Henry Wallace out of the vice-presidential spot and substituting a machine-nurtured candidate from the border state of Missouri. And in 1952 it was the same Southern Democrats who joined with the back-room operators from Chicago, Pittsburgh, and Jersey City in drafting the ultra-smooth Illinois corporation lawyer Adlai E. Stevenson for President in the face of liberal challengers who wanted to boot racist Southerners out of the party.

Needless to add, it was against this combination that the liberal Eugene McCarthy came to grief in the convention of 1968. Southern conservatives are clearly a handy group to have around, especially in a day and age when an attractive liberal Democrat could win a national election fought on bread-and-butter issues.

The importance of Northern machine Democrats to the Southerners who dominate Congress and the middle-of-the-roaders who run for President may come as a shock to many college-educated readers, for they have been assured again and again that the political machine is dead —except, of course, for that awful old vestige of the past, the Daley Machine of Chicago. This alleged death was supposedly traceable to a decline in the importance of patronage jobs, the replacement of local party services to the poor by New Deal welfare programs, and lately to the rise of the "amateur" Democrat, that saint in middle-class armor who fights against the boodle-oriented party drones because of idealistic, issue-oriented motives.

But such claims are primarily wishful thinking based upon a few changes in the Manhattan section of New York and the absence of colorful and well-known bosses —other than Mayor Daley—in large cities. The machines still exist, in some cases strengthened by more lucrative forms of patronage and by the opportunities created for local rake-offs within the welfare provisions of the New Deal. There are times when the machines will lose the mayoralty election, but as one political scientist who studies local government commented to me, "They can indeed control most other city-wide offices and patronages, and also retain a very tenacious base in the central city's congressional districts."

Thus, when liberal columnist Max Lerner announced in 1939 that the day of the "pure politician" like Jim Farley was over and that "today there are new men for new methods—a Hopkins, an Ickes, a Wallace, a Lilienthal, above all a Corcoran," he was contradicted a year later. Boss Ed Flynn of the Bronx was appointed to run Roosevelt's third-term campaign and the Hopkinses and Corcorans fell by the wayside. As a historian of the 1940 campaign was later to write: "If the campaign of 1940 proved anything, however, it was that the day of the 'pure politician' was far from over, and the day of a Hopkins and 'above all a Corcoran' had not yet dawned."

Similarly, when the liberal *New Republic* prophesied in 1949 that the defeat of Frank Hague's nephew as a political boss in New Jersey signaled the end of bossism everywhere, it was merely whistling in the dark, for in 1969 and 1970, newspaper accounts told of scandals and patronage favors involving the party boss, John V. Kenney, who had directed the political machine in Jersey City since he took over as the party's leader in 1949.

The Southern rich have every reason to stay in the Democratic Party, and it seems likely they will be more than welcome there as long as they have the support of their faithful allies—the machine Democrats of Northern cities.

MISSISSIPPI AND THE TRUTH ABOUT THE DEMOCRATS

The Democratic Party will make every effort in the seventies to improve its image by uniting its Northern and Southern wings in harmonious moderation. The Southerners will try to leave the worst forms of racism and extremism to the far-right segregationists who now dominate the GOP in most Southern states, and the Northerners, for their part, will continue to acquiesce in Southern domination of Congress in exchange for pork-barrel favors and help in nominating middle-of-the-road presidential candidates. Along with presenting a more moderate-looking face to the national party, however, the Southern rich will continue to maintain economically conservative regimes on the home front, using racial tactics only when it is necessary to keep the poor whites diverted from economic issues. Most of all, they will continue to look the other way when common decency and civil rights for blacks are at issue. It is in these kinds of arrangements and in out-of-the-way places, not in national images and proclamations about a new harmony, that the truth about the Democratic Party will be found. One such out-of-the-way place is Mississippi.

Mississippi's solidly Democratic delegation to Congress is a hodgepodge of racists and ignoramuses unequaled in its contempt for the party's national platform. Moreover, the seniority of several of its members gives Mississippi influence over legislation of national significance beyond all proportion to the weight of the state in population, wealth, or area. You'd think, then, that reasonable national Democrats would be looking for an excuse to rid their party of this awful blight, forcing it into the ultra-conservative wing of the Republican Party. But, no, the national Democrats have no such intention. "What do they matter?" one Democratic National Committee official asked me in an attempt to express his honest scorn for Mississippi Democrats. "They don't affect anything at the national convention." A party official who is taking a very moderate stance in his own Deep South state also down-played the seeming urgency of doing anything about Mississippi's Democrats. He even argued that it would hurt the party to challenge the Democrats there: "The rest of the South knows that Mississippians are being foolish and stupid, but if you kick them around, you stir up all Southerners. In other words, if you harass Mississippi, you take the chance of losing the South to Wallace and the Republicans all over again."

But Mississippi will not be made to disappear as a Democratic problem by ignoring it. On the contrary, Mississippi is the acid test of the intentions of the Democratic Party as a whole. The way in which the party handled the Mississippi Challenge of January, 1971, does not speak highly of those intentions.

At the 1968 presidential convention a group of black and white leaders were recognized by an overwhelming vote of the delegates as the official Democratic Party in Mississippi. But the white racist Democrats would not allow these loyalist Democrats to list their candidates as Democrats during the 1970 state elections. Nor would they register their own candidates with the loyalist party. As a result, the racists sent a Senator and five Congressmen to Washington who were not legally Democrats. Here was a chance for action. But nothing happened. No one except blacks suggested booting the rebels out of the party. In the Senate, no one even seriously challenged the returning Senator's now-dubious seniority. Over in the House there did arise a tentative "Mississippi Challenge" with the aim of stripping three full-blown racists of their seniority.

But the Democrats in the House would not take this important step, which would have gotten rid of eighty-year-old William M. Colmer as head of the all-powerful Rules Committee, of Jamie Whitten as head of the Agricultural Appropriations Subcommittee, and of Thomas Abernethy as head of the Cotton Subcommittee of House Agriculture. What Whitten and Abernethy do for plantation owners is an outright scandal, but what Colmer does to the nation as a whole is even worse: "He continually blocks important legislation favored by the Democrats," editorialized *The New Republic*. "He refused to allow a rule [a permit for consideration by the whole House] for the equal employment opportunities act of 1970, thus blocking passage of legislation favored by a majority of both houses."

A few House liberals tried to gain support for the challenge by issuing a report showing that there was plenty of precedent for taking seniority away from third-party candidates such as the Mississippi renegades; after all, such had been the fate of eight leftists of varying shades since 1930. But it was not to be the fate of rightists of the most rabid variety. Speaker Carl Albert, the little giant from Oklahoma from whom the slick monthly magazines tell us to expect great things, would have nothing to do with the Challenge. Nor would the fifteen to twenty old bulls who dominate the entire House through its tortuous committee system. Even some of the liberals were scared of it—they knew the many ways the House bosses could hurt them if they chose to do so. At any rate, when all the threatening and promising was completed, the Mississippi Challenge of 1971 received 55 votes.

Yes, only 55 votes out of 254 on the question of taking seniority from three Mississippi racists who repudiate everything the party stands for, block civilized legislation through key committee posts, and don't even belong to the state Democratic Party that was officially recognized by the national party at the 1968 convention. "So," says *Nation* correspondent Robert Sherrill, "if you want to know how many Democrats there are in the U.S. House of Representatives who want to throw off the Southern yoke and free the Rules Committee, there's your answer: fifty-five." It is indeed a revealing answer for those who expect any progressive legislation from the Democratic Party in the near future.

Black Representative John Conyers of Detroit, who engineered the Challenge on behalf of the Mississippi Loyalists, was annoyed by what the outcome revealed. He figures the good ol' boys in the House cloakrooms are telling each other that "We're going to beat Nixon, and screw the blacks at the same time," and that "Our friend-

ship, our loyalty, our camaraderie over these last twenty
to thirty years are far more important than us unifying
the party. . . ." Conyers believes the House leadership
made a big mistake, that it will finally alienate black adults
from the Democratic Party. Conyers may be right, but
with all due respect it should be pointed out that Democrats have been doing the same things with impunity for
years, adopting a pro-civil rights, pro-labor profile in presidential elections (which is the way to beat Nixons), and
voting with the Southerners on the organization of Congress (which is a good way to scuttle middle Americans
as well as blacks).

Another young Congressman, Abner Mikva, one of the
few liberals to make it to Washington from the tightly-
controlled turf of Mayor Richard Daley, also waxed philosophic after the Mississippi Challenge and other disasters
at the opening of the 92nd Congress. His words explain
why Congress, despite a rising number of liberal and middle-ground Democrats in both the Senate and the House,
will transform itself from the inside at a pace that can only
be measured on a geological time scale.

"The biggest single disappointment to a new man is
the intransigence of the system," said Mikva. "You talk
to people and they say, 'You're absolutely right, something ought to be done about this.' And yet, somehow, we
go right on ducking the hard issues. We slide off the necessary confrontations. This place has a way of grinding you
down."

"This place has a way of grinding you down." What a
sad commentary that simple statement is on the system
that the Democratic Party has fashioned to sabotage the
legislative process in the United States.

The Mississippi Challenge of 1971 did not receive

nearly as much publicity as the more dramatic Mississippi Challenges of 1964 and 1965, which also failed as a matter of course. But it reveals the same conservative forces prospering with the Democratic Party, the party which remains in good measure the special hunting ground of the Southern oligarchy.

4

LIMOUSINE LIBERALS

The liberal fringe of the Democratic Party—and it is at best a fringe despite the *majority* support among the American populace for most liberal economic issues—is an unlikely collection of maverick patricians, Jewish millionaires, hired do-gooders, and academic soothsayers who play a complex and contradictory role within a party financially dependent upon moderate Northern Jews at one level and conservative Southern Protestants at another. I say their role is complex and contradictory because they are trying to do so many things at once—to bring improvement in social welfare and civil rights while vehemently defending the basic tenets of the socioeconomic system, to introduce new ideas into the body politic while remaining acceptable to the powers-that-be, to sympathize with the poor while living like kings. The list of ironies is endless. Being a rich liberal is no easy task.

Unlike either Northern kingmakers or Southern subsidy seekers, the wealthy liberals and their entourage do not share business connections. Nor do they emanate from any specific part of the upper crust or corporate community. In fact, except for the expected spillover from the somewhat progressive Jewish communities in New York and Beverly Hills, well-heeled liberals are likely to appear anywhere, and there are so few of them that they are probably best viewed as psychological accidents—people perhaps blessed with an extremely nurturant mother or burdened with a highly developed super ego.

Take the case of Oscar and Andy Carr, millionaire planters in the Mississippi delta. Almost alone among their class, they responded affirmatively to the black struggle for justice, joining the Mississippi Freedom Democratic Party at a time when the people they hobnob with at cotton festivals were becoming even more unreasonable. People like their longtime neighbor who recently served as chairman of the regular Mississippi Democrats just can't understand what got into the Carrs, and the Carrs themselves often wonder why they went one way and their neighbors another. What is clear is that both brothers are deeply religious, principled men whose example has given renewed hope to liberals and racial moderates throughout the South.

Or consider the all-too-brief life of Audrey Bruce Currier. Who would have guessed that the granddaughter of a Scrooge like Andrew Mellon would some day be among the most important financial supporters of liberal Democrats and the movement for civil rights? Or that a General Motors heir and a Singer Sewing Machine heiress would give hundreds of thousands of dollars to the McCarthy campaign in 1968?

Despite their happenstance origins and their lack of corporate interconnections, the leaders of the liberal fringe do tend to know each other rather well, thanks to social and political mingling. They are gathered together in financing and directing a little covey of foundations, think tanks, journals of liberal opinion, and political committees that constitute the liberal cubbyhole within the citadels of the American power elite.

The principal sources of money for the nonpolitical activities of this clique are the New World Foundation, the Field Foundation, the Taconic Foundation, and the Stern Family Fund, with the somewhat more cautious (and richer) Twentieth Century Fund also joining in on occasion. The top think tanks and research outfits of the group, which also function as training grounds and resting spas for liberal activists, are the Center for the Study of Democratic Institutions in Santa Barbara, the Adlai E. Stevenson Institute in Chicago, and the Southern Regional Council in Atlanta.

The benevolent rich among the power elite have several political fronts, most of which serve as support agencies for liberal Democrats even though they remain formally separate from the party and claim to be on the lookout for deserving liberal Republicans. These organizations also are a major avenue by means of which the high-toned liberals relate to their labor-union and middle-class allies. The most muscular of these action arms until recently has been Americans for Democratic Action, which came into existence in 1947 and has set the style in respectable liberal politics ever since. It is a membership organization which lobbies, takes stands on political issues, provides shock troops for liberal causes, and endorses candidates (including Eugene McCarthy after some ambivalence due to the long-standing loyalty of many of its leaders to Hubert Humphrey).

Less well known, but of growing vitality, is the National Committee for an Effective Congress, which had its beginning in 1948. It did not play any lead roles until the midfifties when it helped coordinate the Senate fight (such as it was) against the tirades of Joe McCarthy. Concentrating primarily on foreign policy until recent years, the NCEC really came into its own during the sixties as a dollar funnel that could direct weighty support to liberal Democrats and, occasionally, internationally oriented Republicans.

In 1968, NCEC spokesmen and their favorite money sources were active in the campaign to dump Lyndon Johnson, and in 1970 the NCEC was among the two or three vigorous suppliers of antiwar Senators struggling for survival against the deluge of Republican dollars. Although a few wealthy individuals have helped the organization over financial rough spots, or have used it to pass on donations with which they did not want to be personally identified, most of its cash comes from tantalizing mail appeals to small donors among middle-class liberals. The essential ingredient the propertied liberals lend to the money-raising efforts of NCEC is their nationwide visibility and their establishment credentials.

The informal interconnections of the organizations of the liberal fringe are extensive, particularly in their sources of money. Formal connections are also numerous. For example, corporate lawyer and Democratic trouble-shooter Lloyd K. Garrison of Paul, Weiss, Goldberg, Rifkind, Wharton, and Garrison is a director of both the Field Foundation and the Taconic Foundation. The people who run the New World Foundation also own *The New Republic,* the political magazine most widely read in liberal circles. The Field, New World, Taconic, and Stern foundations provide the Southern Regional Council with the bulk of its financial support. The former research director of the Southern Regional Council, Leslie Dunbar, is now the executive director of the Field Foundation. Hermon D. Smith, insurance executive and lifelong intimate of Adlai E. Stevenson, sits on the boards of the Stevenson Institute and the Field Foundation. ADA leaders John K. Galbraith and Arthur M. Schlesinger, Jr., are directors of the Twentieth Century Fund. Harry Ashmore of the Center for the Study of Democratic Institutions is also a sponsor of the National Committee for an Effective Congress. And all of these groups, in turn, have ties to the liberal and middle-of-the-road tendencies within the Democratic Party. Some, such as the Center for the Study of Democratic Institutions, are well stocked with leading party fat cats. Center directors Howard Stein of the Dreyfus Fund, Stewart Mott, Harold Willens, and Seniel Ostrow were among Eugene McCarthy's largest contributors and fund raisers.

The interlocks within the liberal clique should not leave the mistaken impression that it is an isolated group without personal connections to the more cautious and powerful core of the power elite. Such is not the case. Several of its most visible impresarios are members of the Council on Foreign Relations, for example, and others sit among the anointed of the Committee for Economic Development (the Council on Foreign Relations and the Committee for Economic Development being two of the more strategically situated policy-planning groups of the big-business community). Other directors of liberal organizations have links to the outside world through their involvement with the Carnegie Endowment for International Peace, the Encyclopaedia Britannica, Yale Law School, Simpson, Thacher & Bartlett, and numerous corporations of no small stature. Several of the liberal organizations even include a few Republican directors to add the proper balance.

Through the policies and projects the wealthy liberals finance, they constantly determine the left limit of respectable opinion. They not only encourage mildly innovative ideas, which makes them utterly unique on the American political horizon, but they let the scholars and activists they sustain know when they've gone too far for a liberal clique that has a greater commitment to its fellow rich than it does to social change—by firing them, by cutting off their research support, or by chastising them in articles and speeches as crazy extremists, secret Communists, or impractical idealists. The easing out of overly active intellectual employees at the Center for the Study of Democratic Institutions, in 1969, and the Adlai E. Stevenson Institute, in 1970, are only two of the more recent instances of what happens to those who venture too far for the tastes of conventional liberals. Most limousine liberals want a little touching up of the socioeconomic system around the ragged edges, but they don't want anybody tampering with sacred corporate institutions.*

* One of the interviews for this book, with a person who gave tens of thousands of dollars to Eugene McCarthy in 1968, was actually held in a gigantic Rolls-Royce after a restaurant setting became too noisy. The person is noted for telling one egalitarian activist that "Some things wouldn't be any fun if everyone had money," which is probably the kind of remark that led working-class Democrats in New York to coin the phrase "limousine liberal."

What are the inviolable Left Gates that the establishment liberals so faithfully guard? To look at the careers and speeches of the most noted centurions, you'd think they were merely against Communism, which doesn't seem very unusual, since just about everybody in the USA who is over thirty-five (the age limit keeps going up all the time) is alert against the Red Menace and the Yellow Peril.

But when we probe a little deeper, it turns out that any new social policy the liberal rich and their academic admirers don't like is attacked as Communism. What the limousine liberals are thereby able to help defend are two of the most important policies of the entire power elite: an interventionist, big-business-oriented foreign policy, and the discouragement of nationwide third parties. To be against American foreign policy—which defends the status quo everywhere in the "free world," no matter what the status quo may be—or to start a third party is clearly forbidden.

The present-day liberal guardians won their spurs fighting these two issues between 1946 and 1948, for it was in those years that there were vehement arguments over the pros and cons of trying to come to an accommodation with the Soviet Union and over the advisability of starting a liberal third party to compete with the racist-ridden Democrats. The most tangible results of power-elite victories on these issues were the destruction of the Progressive Party and the enshrinement of the hard-line foreign policy being perpetrated by Democrats James Forrestal of Dillon, Read and the Defense Department, Averell Harriman of Brown Brothers, Harriman and the Commerce Department, and Dean Acheson of Covington and Burling and the State Department.

The forties may seem like ancient history to some readers, and many Cold-War liberals have changed their views somewhat in the ensuing years, but the story of establishment liberalism in the postwar years is worth the telling because it is the most important recent example of how the liberal clique works to keep possible social change within conventional limits.

THE DEFENDERS OF THE LEFT FLANK

Because American Communists were under orders from Moscow to support liberals during most of the years between 1935 and 1945, it had become difficult for some people to distinguish liberals from revolutionaries. It was especially hard for ultra-conservatives, who have difficulty with subtle distinctions anyhow, and the mixing of liberals, socialists, and Communists in many of the same organizations made them very nervous. Fortunately, the outlook cleared somewhat in early 1947 when prominent liberal Democrats, many of them patrician gentiles who had been high-level brass in the New Deal, joined with anticommunist union leaders in forming an organization known as Americans for Democratic Action (hereafter ADA). It was designed to check the leftward drift of certain wealthy eccentrics and misguided middle-class liberals who were working in conjunction with Communists in challenging the get-tough foreign policy and in organizing a progressive third party. This noncommunist organization, as these liberals preferred to refer to it, has been the watchtower for socially acceptable liberalism ever since. Politically speaking, its history embodies the main outlines of liberalism in the postwar years.

The ADA was formed in the first week of January, 1947,

at a meeting of four hundred liberals and labor leaders in Washington, D.C. Among the primary sponsors were theologian Reinhold Niebuhr, Mrs. Eleanor Roosevelt, former Attorney General Francis Biddle, former OPA chieftain Leon Henderson, former Housing Expediter Wilson Wyatt, union leaders and other wheeler-dealers who had been adamant in their opposition to a coexistence foreign policy, third parties, and working with American Communists. Indeed, the formation of ADA was in good part a response to the development during 1946 of a group known as Progressive Citizens of America, a collection of middle-class liberals and Communists who believed that America's hard-line foreign policy was more responsible for U.S.–Soviet differences than was Stalin. Moreover, many members of the PCA group had hopes of starting a third party on the coattails of a presidential candidacy by Henry A. Wallace. Wallace, who was Roosevelt's Secretary of Agriculture (1933–40) and Vice-President (1941–45), had been ousted from the post of Secretary of Commerce by Truman in September, 1946, for his disagreements with the administration's attitude toward Russia.

The theme of the ADA meeting was set forth in a speech by New Dealer Chester Bowles, one of the wealthy founders (along with fellow Democrat William Benton) of the Benton and Bowles advertising agency. Bowles announced it was essential to "organize a progressive front, divorced from Communist influence." However, he warned the faithful "not to harbor any illusions about a third party." They should work within the Democratic Party despite its racist Southern anchor. "We cannot blink the fact that the party of Roosevelt is also the party of Bilbo and Rankin," he intoned. "But the fact remains that we have no practical alternative. All our efforts, all

our ingenuity must be thrown into the struggle to establish liberal control of the Democratic Party."

The primary substantive difference between ADA and
PCA as they hurled speeches and news releases back and
forth during 1947 was on foreign policy. ADA embarrass-
edly backed the Truman doctrine and PCA attacked it.
ADA eagerly endorsed the Marshall Plan, which claimed
lofty social and economic benefits as well as obvious geo-
political goals, and the PCA criticized it as a prop for
reactionary governments with far-flung colonial empires.
The two groups also skirmished on the third-party question, with some PCA luminaries hinting at such a course
and almost all ADA people vigorously opposing it.

When Wallace finally announced his presidential candidacy on a "New Party" ticket in late 1947, the battle
between the ADA and the PCA was fully joined. Now the
two-party system as well as the aggressive foreign policy
was being challenged, and everyone in the liberal community was forced to choose sides. Indeed, some liberals
within PCA who had been using it as a pressure group
against the Democrats, or as a platform for a campaign
within the Democratic Party by Wallace, went over to the
ADA side. A few did so with a parting shot at "communist" influences on the third-party decision. It was to be a
mean and unprincipled battle, with the issue of the nature
and intent of U.S. foreign policy almost completely lost in
the charges about communist infiltration.

The ADA opened its broadside against Wallace during
its first national convention in early 1948, asserting that
"It is an established fact that it [the Progressive Party]
owes its origin and principal organizational support to
the Communist Party of America." This claim about "established facts" far overshadowed in sensationalism sup-

port for the Marshall Plan and the other substantial reasons why the liberal Democrats were implacable enemies of Wallace and the new party.

Charges of communist inspiration for the Wallace party had appeared from time to time in the press prior to the ADA announcement. In June, 1947, for instance, A. A. Berle, Jr., a wealthy corporation lawyer for sugar interests, and majordomo of the Liberal Party in New York, had claimed that the PCA was "an appeasement party" led by "American Communists and fellow travelers, acting in accord with their Moscow correspondents," and in December of the same year columnist Stewart Alsop, a founding member of ADA, had written that "The Wallace third party movement has been indecently exposed for what it is: an instrument of Soviet foreign policy." However, the ADA resolution was really the start of the all-out campaign to tar-and-feather Wallace, and it was followed by a widely circulated ADA pamphlet full of innuendos and half-truths about the role of Communists in the origins of the party. Most of the various charges were indeed nasty, especially coming from principled liberals of the highest moral persuasions. And most of them were distortions when they were not outright falsehoods.

Henry Wallace himself and a handful of his noncommunist friends, a few of them quite wealthy, were the crucial factors in the decision to launch the Progressive Party. They set the policies. They raised the lion's share of the money. (More than $800,000 of the $1.8 million spent on the national level came from one super-wealthy widow, Mrs. Anita McCormick Blaine, who admired Wallace personally.) They gave the party whatever visibility, respectability, and appeal it attained.

That Communists were present was no secret, and they

lent their efforts to gathering petitions, raising money, and serving in office positions, but they did not have the role ADA attributed to them. Indeed, Wallace's refusal to "denounce" or "repudiate" his Communist supporters, as the ADA constantly challenged him to do, was not because he thought he needed them. If anything, he thought they were a liability. His refusal to denounce Communists was based on his overwhelming concern for a peaceful solution to American-Soviet differences. A repudiation of the American Communists would have implied it was not possible to work with Communists. "The props would have been knocked out from under Wallace's arguments as to what American foreign policy should be," writes his most sympathetic critic, Curtis D. MacDougall, in a three-volume history of the Progressive Party which deals effectively with the accusations about communist domination. "He would have had little basis for his criticism of the Truman Doctrine, the Marshall Plan, and other aspects of the United States strategy in the Cold War."

But a more balanced perspective on the communist question hardly would have been of much use for political purposes. If the bipartisan foreign policy, with attendant corporate expansion all over the globe, was to receive acquiescence without serious discussion, and the Wallace vote kept as low as possible so he would not cost Truman any of the large states, it was better to picture Wallace as "adopted by Communists," "dupe of Reds," and other such bogeyman charges. As Wallace well knew, the communist issue was a dodge of the important questions which were never faced.

In undertaking the hatchet job on Wallace, an axing that included character assassination as well as red smearing, the ADA was playing the part assigned to liberal

Democrats by Truman's campaign mastermind, Clark Clifford, one of the few Truman aides who even remotely fitted the designation "liberal." In November, 1947, Clifford had drawn up a detailed plan for the 1948 campaign. It included special emphasis on civil rights, organized labor, and liberal domestic issues, a strategy expressly designed, to quote from the document itself, "not only to embarrass the Republicans but to steal Henry Wallace's thunder, for if Wallace drew enough votes, especially in the West, he would defeat Truman." There was also stress on anticommunism in order to hold the Catholic vote, for Clifford believed "The controlling element in this group . . . is the distrust and fear of communism. . . ."

As part of the anticommunist strategy, there was to be a big flap over the alleged communist origins of the Wallace candidacy, but such claims were to be left expressly to the liberals. "To undercut Wallace's appeal," explained analyst Irwin Ross, "Clifford urged that at the psychologically correct moment the communist inspiration behind Wallace's campaign should be denounced by [to quote Clifford] 'prominent liberals and progressives—*and no one else.*'" In all this conniving, Clifford showed remarkable foresight, especially in that Communists did not become active as behind-the-scenes pushers of a Wallace candidacy until about the time Clifford was developing the campaign strategy. There is thus no reason to doubt that Clifford was worth every penny of the hundreds of thousands of dollars in retainer fees that he commanded from large corporations when he settled down to a private law practice in Washington.

The ADA, of course, hardly won the battle against Wallace by itself. Far from it. The primary credit goes to Truman and Clifford, who ran a give-'em-hell whistle-stop campaign that came down hard on the bread-and-butter issues of concern to the workingman. Then, too, the proper dosages of fear and intimidation were injected by the roughhouse tactics of right-wing Catholic trade unionists, veterans' committees, congressional investigating committees, and local authorities. Nevertheless, friends and critics of ADA agree it played a potent role within liberal and labor circles. "In many quarters," says one ADA critic who worked in the Progressive Party, "red-baiting from liberals carries much more weight; and it was in such quarters that the ADA was effective against the Wallaceites."

Despite the ADA's yeoman guerrilla warfare in denouncing Wallace and silencing criticism of the interventionist foreign policy which has consolidated America's enormous informal empire, it did not gain great favor with President-elect Harry S Truman. Lest he seem like an ingrate, it must be added that ADA had worked as hard to depose him as it had worked to discredit Wallace. In one of the most amusing—and unprincipled—adventures in ADA history, the group had schemed to replace Truman with none other than Dwight David Eisenhower, the fatherly general about whose principles, let alone party affiliation, little was known. A few liberal ideologists felt there was a certain danger in ADA's "panting after a candidate about whom it knows no more than that he has a marked humanitarianism, a warm smile, and an excellent chance of winning an election," but such qualms quickly passed.

Among the first Democrats who climbed aboard the artfully orchestrated ADA bandwagon were the Southerners, a curious turn of events if it were not known that two of the few political tidbits extant about Ike were his partiality to states' rights and segregation in the Army. Even a well-oiled machine Democrat, Jake Arvey of Chicago, expressed interest. By the time of the 1948 convention it looked as though ADA's own general had more than 200 votes in the South along with 36 votes delivered by courtesy of the guileless Democratic boss of New Jersey, Frank Hague.

Alas, Ike was not interested. He sent telegram after telegram of refusal, and even resisted an ADA motorcade to his very doorstep. A last-ditch effort to switch the anti-Truman claque to Supreme Court Justice William Douglas was unsuccessful, and the would-be kingmakers had to retire to their more traditional roles as supporting actors.

The history of Americans for Democratic Action has been more prosaic since the forties, so it need receive only brief attention. During the fifties it served primarily as a scapegoat for right-wing Republicans, some of whom claimed it was really an offshoot of the Progressive Citizens of America, the very organization ADA had denounced so bitterly during 1947 and 1948. With the election of John F. Kennedy, however, ADA achieved new heights of respectability. Many of its founding members received positions in second- and third-line garrisons of the New Frontier. But the Johnson Administration, despite the social reforms it sponsored, was not a time of great influence for the waning ADA.

By 1967 the seriousness of the Sino–Soviet split, the political caution of the Soviet Politburo, the stagnation of the Soviet economy, the destruction of the Communist Party in Indonesia, and several other changes in the world situation permitted the establishment-oriented liberals suddenly and incisively to see the Vietnam War as a mistake that could be blamed on little bureaucratic blunders and bad advice from the military and CIA. This penetrat-

ing insight in turn freed those ADA leaders not committed
to Hubert Humphrey to join eagerly in the search for a
successor to Johnson.

Today, its internal disagreements over the Vietnam War
largely forgotten, Americans for Democratic Action continues to struggle along in its multiple roles of innovator,
guardian, and scapegoat with good-humored forbearance.

THE LIBERALS AND THE SOUTH

In the postwar era, but certainly not before, one of the
concerns of well-fixed liberal Democrats has been civil
rights for blacks. The ADA—in part to undercut Henry
Wallace further—pressed for a strong civil-rights plank in
the 1948 Democratic platform, and since at least the mid-
fifties the liberal fringe has been using its foundations to
undermine segregation in the South. Among the rights the
liberals would like to see Southern blacks obtain is the
right to vote, which could potentially have some little
effect on the Southern Democrats and the conservative
coalition within Congress.

Needless to say, then, the efforts of the liberal fringe in
this direction have not endeared them to Dixie politicians.
In fact, their challenges to the Southern way of life have
created tensions which help to make the Democratic Party
the neurotic beast that it is. Once again, however, the
limousine liberals have shown there are severe limits to
what they will tolerate. Some blacks, as we will see, went
beyond the pale in their enthusiasm, and the result has
been their banishment for alleged involvement in com
munist conspiracies.

The major Southern staging ground for the Northern
liberals has been the Southern Regional Council, an At-

lanta-based organization that specializes in research, education, consultation, and discussion groups in order to bring justice to the Negro in the South. Founded in 1944 by black educators and white liberals of middle-class backgrounds, its history was a rocky one until Northern foundations began to support its programs, turning the modest council into one of the most visible and pointed spokesmen for civil rights in the South. The biggest infusion of money came from the Fund for the Republic, a charitable organization concerned with civil liberties and civil rights which had been created with a $15 million grant from the Ford Foundation. The Fund was a source of great consternation to conservatives because of its programs to combat Joe McCarthyism, blacklisting, and other mental aberrations of the fifties. Its initial beneficence to the Southern Regional Council was for $240,000 in 1954. This was followed up with several other hefty gifts over the next three years for a grand total of $750,000, making it possible for the council to expand its program, including human-rights councils, into every state in the South.

In 1956 the Fund was joined in its Southern efforts by the New World Foundation, which picked up the tab for an enlarged format for the council's magazine, *New South*. When the Fund went out of the granting business in the late fifties to concentrate on thinking and talking (under the heady designation "Center for the Study of Democratic Institutions") in a posh mansion in the hills above Santa Barbara, the Field, Taconic, and Stern foundations increased their donations to the council. No Southern foundation except that of the Sterns jumped at the chance to show its commitment to higher aspirations, however. In fact, to this day the council has received only one grant—for $50,000 in 1967—from a Southern-based foundation other than the Stern Family Fund. Nor has the council ever enjoyed the personal largesse of any of the wealthy families of the South with the exception of the Sterns of New Orleans.

The quiet work of the Southern Regional Council, the NAACP, and other organizations looked after by Northern liberals was interrupted in February, 1960, when the era of black activism began suddenly and spontaneously with a sit-in by four black collegians at a whites-only lunch counter in Greensboro, North Carolina. The sit-in movement spread quickly, and soon led to Freedom Rides to break segregation in buses and bus terminals. By the summer of 1961 young activists from all over the South were meeting regularly as members of the Student Non-Violent Coordinating Committee (SNCC).

It was into this ferment that the liberals and their foundations hastily entered with the promise of lots of money if the students would only turn their energies to a voter-registration drive. The liberals, it was claimed, were happy to see the black insurgency. But they did not want the uprising to expand outside the pathways that had been developed patiently by their largesse during the late fifties. They were not prepared to support the alternative, nonviolent tactics that had broken the longstanding pattern of inaction in the South.

The cash offer was made through a bright young black, Tim Jenkins, who was the vice-president of the National Student Association.

> Even before the Freedom Rides began [wrote historian Howard Zinn, who was teaching in Atlanta at the time], Jenkins had been attending a series of meetings in which representatives of several foun-

dations, including the Taconic and Field foundations, discussed the raising of substantial funds to
support a large-scale voter registration effort in the
South. Present at those meetings were Burke Marshall, Assistant Attorney General in charge of the
Civil Rights Division [a former member of the
Washington law firm of Covington and Burling,
now the general counsel for IBM], and Harris
Wofford, special assistant to President Kennedy on
civil rights. Jenkins was asked by the Foundation
people to broach the idea to his friends in SNCC.

The foundation offer started a controversy within the
Student Non-Violent Coordinating Committee that almost split the group asunder. The direct-action advocates
were suspicious of the offer, especially considering the
fact that Attorney General Robert F. Kennedy had quickly
called for a "cooling-off" period during the Freedom
Rides. As the Southern Regional Council reported in a
1963 issue of *New South,* "During the late spring and
summer of 1961, it was hardly a secret that the Department of Justice was among those quietly, but strongly,
urging this [voter registration] emphasis." The issue was
finally resolved with a compromise—SNCC would do
both direct action and voter registration. Several SNCC
leaders had been thinking about the possibility of voter
registration anyhow, so a crisis was averted, at least for
the time being. What directions SNCC would have taken
if left to itself will never be known, but the attempt by the
limousine liberals to keep things within the channels they
prefer is rather apparent. Their money, as always, had
strings attached to it. They were attempting to define the
limits of acceptable civil rights activity.

With the SNCC decision to push into voter registration, Northern liberal money came raining down. By 1967
the Taconic Foundation had given $339,000, the Field
Foundation $225,000, and the Stern Family Fund $219,000
for the voter program. It was this money that financed,
among many things, the famous Mississippi Freedom
Summer of 1964. However, the foundations did not give
the money to SNCC directly. Instead, they passed it to
the Southern Regional Council, which then handed it out
to a variety of black civil-rights groups through a new
Voter Education Project. The council, of course, was
the ideal vehicle for coordinating the voter drive. It had
respectability, a tax-exempt status, information, an exper-
ienced staff, and contacts all over the South—thanks in
good part to the energizing effects of Northern liberal
money. Although many conservatives were distraught,
particularly Southern conservatives, fence sitters and liberals knew that affairs were in reliable hands.

Money for registering blacks did not come solely from
foundations. Much also came from the personal pocket-
books of handsomely endowed liberals, and from middle-
grounders who could be tapped by properly credentialed
liberals. The man who played the critical role in this personal equation was one of the founders of the Taconic
Foundation, Stephen Currier. Currier's most famous
money-raising event was a New York breakfast in June,
1963, for civil-rights leaders and ninety-six corporation
and foundation officials. A whopping $800,000 was there
pledged to a new United Council on Civil Rights that
was to be cochaired by Currier and Whitney Young of the
Urban League.

As usual, the concern appeared to be as much in mod-
erating the new activists as it was in supporting them.
There was talk, for instance, of "more professional leader-

ship to prevent violence," talk which did not have the right ring for nonviolent activists who felt the best way to prevent violence was not to infuse their movement with "professional leadership," but to restrain the segregationists who were guilty of the violence. Similarly, a report on the goals of Currier and his friends suggests the establishment liberals' misplaced emphasis concerning the most effective way to deal with violence in the civil rights struggle. "In encouraging funds for the 'action' organizations, especially," wrote journalist Reese Cleghorn in the *New Republic* in 1963, "Currier is said to have had his eye upon the demonstrations taking place, often *without firm direction* [my italics–GWD]. Much of this money will be used to add to the professional staffs of the participants. It is not truly a case of infiltrating the revolution with money, the sponsors insist."

Very few people ever heard of Stephen Currier, but they would have if he had lived his normal life span. He was the wealthiest liberal of his generation. It is one of the great misfortunes of modern liberalism that he and his wife did not live to carry out their plan to devote the income from their enormous fortune to charitable and liberal causes.

Currier was the stepson of Edward M. M. Warburg of the Kuhn, Loeb banking family. His wife was the daughter of Democratic diplomat David K. E. Bruce and Republican centimillionaire Ailsa Mellon, the wealthiest woman in America. When the couple married in the mid-fifties, they had between them several million dollars, and they were determined to use it for service to liberal programs. One of their first acts was to set up the Taconic Foundation, which soon involved itself in civil rights, giving over a million dollars to that struggle between 1960 and 1963.

But that was only to be the beginning, for Mrs. Currier was to inherit over $500 million, one of the largest fortunes in America, when her mother passed away! And the Curriers intended to utilize the tax-protected income from that stupendous sum of money, an income which would be in the tens of millions of dollars each year, for a wide range of political and charitable purposes. The line-up included the Taconic Foundation (their instrument for aiding civil rights), the Potomac Institute (their institute for the study of race relations), Urban America (their institute for aiding the cities), and the Democratic Party (their instrument for changing America).

The seriousness of their interest in liberal politics is indicated by their hiring of George Agree, the veteran executive director of the National Committee for an Effective Congress, as the full-time manager of their political money. It was to be his sole job to decide how best to donate $100,000 a year to political candidates, and that figure was scheduled to be increased substantially when Mrs. Currier came into the rest of her inheritance. It looked as though liberals were finally going to be able to get somewhere close to conservatives and reactionaries in campaign spending. Already in the midsixties the Curriers were among the Democrats' largest bankrollers.

The Curriers worked quietly. There was nothing strange or unusual about them. They were on good personal terms with their Mellon relatives. They shunned publicity, and often operated through spokesmen. Even their philanthropies outside of civil rights were unusual. "They never gave a dime to a building [to be named for them], they only gave to people and programs—they spent time finding out for themselves what they wanted to support," said one Currier adviser. Among non-Taconic donations totaling $767,000 was $100,000 to a group opposing a proposed Consolidated Edison power plant on the Hudson River.

The great potential of the Curriers was not to be realized, for they were killed in early 1967 in the crash of the private plane they had chartered in their eagerness to return to New York from San Juan, Puerto Rico, to see their children in a school performance. Mrs. Currier's mother died two years later, but the $500 million-plus the Curriers were to receive is now tied up in trust funds for the children, and the thrust of the Taconic Foundation, the Potomac Institute, and Urban America has been severely blunted. It is not often that the death of two people can be said to make such a difference, but $40–60 million a year would have been a tremendous transfusion for the anemic liberal fringe.

The money rounded up by Currier and the liberal foundations in the early sixties financed one of the most harrowing and tragic experiments of recent times, the influx of thousands of Northern white students into Mississippi during the summer of 1964 in an attempt to crack the staunchest segregationist state in the nation. Leading the black activists of SNCC vintage was Bob Moses, who had come to the South from New York as part of the movement generated by the sit-ins. Through his long service in Mississippi he had become a legend among youth for his quiet and courageous work under the worst conditions. Leading the whites was Allard Lowenstein, a thirty-five-year-old lawyer and ADA liberal who had been involved in liberal causes since his youth. Through his involvement in the National Student Association, which went back to his election to its presidency in 1951, Lowenstein was able to bring thousands of white collegians to Mississippi to help the SNCC activists.

One of Lowenstein's ideas had been to start a Missis-

sippi Freedom Democratic Party to bypass the white segregationist party. The plan caught on, and soon many
blacks were deeply involved. But the direction the party
took soon led to conflict between Moses and Lowenstein.
Moses saw the party as a means by which poor blacks
could become involved in the political process whereas
Lowenstein apparently saw it as something that might
hook up with liberal Democrats in the North. "To Al,"
according to one of his friends of that time, "the FDP
represented a temporary device as much as a permanent
organization: he was as eager for it to gain substantial
support in white Washington as in black Mississippi,
thought that it might even give integrationists like Ed
King, Aaron Henry, and Charles Evers enough leverage to
reform the regular Democratic Party."

A "radical" versus "liberal" argument slowly developed
between Moses and Lowenstein. Unfortunately, Lowenstein felt there was more to it than that. He began to
wonder whether the hand of Communism might be lurk-
ing behind the concern with participatory democracy es-
poused by Moses and his fellow black activists. "There
was a simple pattern to his disclosures," says the same
friend. "Evil people had gained control of a movement
that promised to do much good for America, and the innocent black peasants and misguided white students had
to be saved from the Communists."

The behavior of the Freedom Democrats at the 1964
Democratic Convention led to further antagonisms between the black activists and the liberals, for the blacks
refused to accept the compromise of only two voting delegates offered to them when they challenged the right of
the racist regulars to be seated as acceptable participants.
The Freedom Democrats, who had announced their sup-

port of the party platform and expressed their willingness to sign an oath swearing fealty to the national party, could not agree that they should receive only two delegate seats when the regular party was frankly segregationist, antagonistic to the party platform, on record against the Civil Rights Act of 1964, and openly supportive of Governor George Wallace of Alabama.

The Freedom Democrats' intransigence annoyed the establishment liberals. Among other things, many of them feared that ADA charter member Hubert Humphrey's place on the ticket was dependent upon a satisfactory resolution of the Mississippi controversy. Thus, it is not surprising that Humphrey and another ADA leader, lawyer Joseph Rauh, who was serving as a consultant to the Mississippi Freedom Democratic Party, did everything they could to smooth the situation over by trying to induce the upstart blacks to accept the unbalanced compromise. One leader of the Freedom Democrats reported that "Mr. Humphrey, he kept telling us to compromise for two votes. He seemed *very* upset, very upset. Our attorney at the time [Rauh] told us if we didn't go for the two votes, if we didn't *slow down,* Mr. Humphrey wouldn't get the nomination. I declare it was Mr. Rauh, and that's what he said. Mr. Humphrey was sitting right there when Mr. Rauh said that and he had tears in his eyes—I mean Humphrey had tears in his eyes—when Joe Rauh said it." *

Rauh and other ADA liberals were hurt and angry when the Mississippi blacks rejected their advice. They couldn't imagine that the blacks made their own decision

---

* Readers should not be disturbed by Humphey's tears. He can cry very readily, and does so on all necessary occasions.

in their own best interests. They began to suspect, like
Lowenstein, who to his credit remained neutral in the
delegate fight, that something fishy might be going on in
the civil-rights movement. "They couldn't believe," says
Paul Cowan, the former friend of Al Lowenstein already
quoted, "that the Mississippians had rationally decided to
reject their advice. So the liberals began to argue that
poor black people had been duped by SNCC staff members whose interests had nothing to do with their own:
men with un-American ideas who had worked their way
into the movement's leadership and craftily managed to
win the confidence of the unsophisticated."

The notion that the black civil-rights activists were
Communist-influenced once again suggests a characteristic reaction on the part of establishment-oriented liberals
and their wealthy backers. Anybody concerned with social change who doesn't agree with the goals and strategies developed with the financial aid of limousine liberals
must be a Communist, or at least communist-influenced.
One of Lowenstein's friends probably captured general
establishment liberal psychology on this score when he
told journalist David Halberstam, "That's his [Lowen-
stein's] great strength, talking to these clean-cut young
kids, getting them back into the system. He doesn't work
nearly as well to the left, and he loses patience; it's as if
he doesn't think people have the right to be to the left of
him. Al likes to start things, but when they get out of
hand and get revolutionary, he doesn't like it."

The conflict at the 1964 Democratic Convention, as
might be expected, deeply embittered many young blacks.
Some SNCC leaders turned to Black Power and greater
militancy. Others, such as Bob Moses, dropped out of the
movement in despair. A few threw in their lot with the
Southern Regional Council. As for the rich Northern lib-

erals, most of them withdrew their personal financial support from SNCC, partly because of what they heard from Lowenstein about the Mississippi Summer, partly because of the embarrassing events at the Democratic Convention. It was the beginning of the end for SNCC.

However, despite the parting of the ways with SNCC, the limousine liberals did not abandon their commitment to voter registration, which had been their original objective anyhow as the magic formula (along with education and legal challenges) for helping Southern blacks achieve equal opportunity. Liberal foundations continued to pour money into the Southern Regional Council and the NAACP Legal Defense Fund in grants that often ran into the hundreds of thousands of dollars. In 1966, the Southern Regional Council even received $300,000 from the Ford Foundation after a public nudging by Philip Stern of the Stern Family Fund. A listing of some of the 1968–69 civil-rights grants by the Field Foundation, a $38 million treasure trove, is indicative of the liberal impetus toward racial equality in the South through establishment-certified channels:

Selected Field Foundation Grants for 1968–69

$ 588,000	Southern Regional Council
$ 435,000	NAACP Legal Defense and Education Funds
$ 85,000	Friends of Children of Mississippi (pre-schools)
$ 80,000	Appalachian Volunteers
$ 40,000	Alabama Council on Human Relations (an SRC creation)
$ 33,800	Committee of Southern Churchmen
$1,261,800	TOTAL

So the liberal commitment to bringing civil rights to the South is deadly serious despite the disturbances it causes within the Democratic Party. It has cost many millions of dollars, and it may encourage Southern Democrats to mend some of their coarser ways. On the other hand, the commitment of the limousine liberals decidedly does not include a direct challenge to the national Democratic Party, to leaders of ADA, or, for that matter, to any American institution that is cherished by the enlightened rich.

THE TURF OF THE LIBERALS

The liberal fringe of the Democratic Party is no mere tangle of foundations, think tanks, and ADA chapters serving as gadfly or guardian on vital issues like foreign policy, civil rights, and, belatedly, peace in Vietnam. It is also the financial and ideological cockpit for a liberal movement that has a territorial base in a handful of urban centers and in several Midwestern and Western states. It was this movement, underwritten of course by the usual wealthy benefactors, that put together the Eugene McCarthy challenge of 1968. A brief examination of the liberal presence in two major breeding grounds further reveals the extent of the liberal potential within the Democratic Party.*

Michigan provides the case of a Democratic Party run by limousine liberals with the support of organized labor.

---

* Actually, the McCarthy campaign of 1968 also had the largesse of several wealthy people new to politics, and of two or three free-spending Republicans who passionately disliked the war. This said, however, the movers and shakers of the enterprise were well-worn members of the liberal fringe.

In this state, which is every Republican's favorite bogey-man example of labor "domination" in the Democratic Party, the liberal-labor alliance dates from November, 1947, when wealthy lawyers G. Mennen Williams (of the Mennen shaving-soap family) and Hicks G. Griffiths joined with union leaders, particularly those within the United Auto Workers, to regenerate a decrepit party structure which had not yet fully assimilated the recently organized CIO unions. The auto workers, some of whom had been toying with the idea of third-party politics, provided some of the money and most of the votes, "Soapy" Williams and his friends provided respectability, ideas, leadership, and money. Among the Williams friends in the new coalition were Hickman Price, president of Kaiser-Frazer, Neil Staebler, a wealthy Ann Arbor businessman, and Philip Hart, whose wife was of the super-wealthy Briggs family of Detroit.

Running on ADA-type platforms, and with the solid backing of labor, it did not take the liberals long to gain important offices in the Republican-dominated state. Williams became governor for a record-breaking six straight terms (1949–1961), Mrs. Hicks Griffiths has been seated in the House of Representatives since 1954. Philip Hart was elected to the Senate in 1958, and Neil Staebler was state party chairman from 1950 to 1961. Not that labor people were denied office; James O'Hara, for instance, is an influential member of the House of Representatives with thirteen years of seniority. He is considered labor's man within the halls of Congress when it comes to leadership.

Wisconsin presents a more unusual arrangement. There the party was rejuvenated by LaFollette Progressives, ex-socialists, and liberal Democrats led by a patrician car-

petbagger who had been headed for a banking career with
J. P. Morgan & Company when World War II interrupted
his plans. As in Michigan, the resurgence of the party was
a phenomenon of the forties. It began in 1946 when a
number of Progressive Republicans, including now-Sena-
tor Gaylord Nelson, came over to the Democrats rather
than align themselves with the kind of Republican Party
that had sent Joe McCarthy to the Senate.

One of the essential people in rebuilding the party in
Wisconsin was William Proxmire, who moved to the state
in the late forties expressly for the purpose of becoming
a politician. Proxmire was a prototype of the patrician
convert so conspicuous on the liberal fringe. The scion
of a conservative, Socially Registered Republican family,
he had attended the exclusive Hill School in Pottstown,
Pennsylvania, before going on to Yale and Harvard Business School. Following that he went to Wall Street and
joined J. P. Morgan & Company (by then he was married
to a Rockefeller of Standard Oil money). The war dis-
rupted his business career, and when it ended, he left
Army Intelligence for further study at Harvard. Proxmire
soon decided on a political career, and on Wisconsin, with
its progressive tradition and newly-activated Democratic
Party, as the most likely state in which to launch it. Arriv-
ing in Wisconsin, he worked for a time as a reporter for
the liberal Madison *Capitol-Times,* then moved on to the
Union Labor News. All the while he was involved with
the liberals, ex-progressives, and ex-socialists who in 1949
had formed the Democratic Organizing Committee as the
first step in putting new life into what had been until
then the third party in Wisconsin.

After winning a seat in the state legislature in 1950,
Proxmire ran for governor in 1952, receiving a meager

thirty-seven percent of the vote. He again ran unsuccessfully in 1954 and 1956, each time becoming more visible and respectable by means of nonstop handshaking throughout the state. Following the 1956 loss and a divorce, he married an officer of the state party and settled down to managing a printing business. But with the death of Senator Joe McCarthy in May, 1957, there was the need for a Democratic candidate in the special statewide election, and Proxmire was off and running. To everyone's amazement, he won the special election, then returned a year later to win his own six-year term with fifty-seven percent of the vote. He is now considered one of the leading mavericks in the Senate, but remains well-liked in his state even by critics because he "talks like a Republican" (which probably means with proper patrician cool) and fights against government waste (particularly in the Pentagon). Since Proxmire's victory Wisconsin Democrats have had other liberal successes. For example, Gaylord Nelson won the governorship in 1958 and went to the Senate in 1962, while the present Governor, Patrick J. Lucey, is one of a handful of liberal Catholics visible in the national party.

Proxmire's uphill election fight of 1958 brought to the surface the kind of financial in-fighting that goes on between liberals and conservatives within the national party. The conservatives were not pleased to be joined in the Senate by the likes of Proxmire, especially after he joined the effort to reduce the oil depletion tax allowance from twenty-seven and a half percent to fifteen percent. So the Democratic Senatorial Campaign Committee, guided by conservatives Lyndon Johnson of Texas and George Smathers of Florida, awarded Proxmire a paltry $1,100 from its oil-drenched war chest for his re-election campaign. Conservative Democratic candidates fared much, much better: several hundred thousand dollars were reportedly given to them. The senatorial campaign of Governor Edmund Muskie of Maine was sent $90,000 according to one account.

When news of this gross favoritism reached the offices of the National Committee for an Effective Congress, its angry leaders rolled out their heaviest weapon. They wrote one of their "Berle Letters," a device reserved only for the most critical of circumstances. By a Berle Letter they meant a desperate plea for money written on the stationery of none other than the late Wall Street lawyer and author, A. A. Berle, Jr.

But the clout was not Berle's alone despite his multimillionaire standing. It was signed by Jacob M. Kaplan, the former president of Welch Grape Juice and one of the party's easiest marks for twenty-five years—including at least $15,500 in 1968. Then there was Angier Biddle Duke, with Democratic credentials deep in Philadelphia history and money even deeper into Southern tobacco country. Also lending his great prestige was Sidney H. Scheuer, whose concern is an international textile business when he is not tending to NCEC affairs. Finally, for appeal to a little different crowd, there was the signature of Oscar Hammerstein II.

The Berle Letter, clearly a collector's item if there ever was one, was hurriedly shot out to all those optimistic souls in the New York metropolitan area who had unburdened themselves of $500 or more for the candidacy of Adlai E. Stevenson in 1956. One result was a number of financial contributions for Proxmire. Even more importantly, the embarrassed Democratic Senate Campaign

Committee kicked in a substantial amount for Proxmire and other liberal Senatorial aspirants.

The Wisconsin story also casts light on the general picture of campaign finance, because it was the subject of one of the most thorough studies ever made of this taboo topic. The investigator, David Adamany, was both a political scientist and a political insider who had served on the staff of Democratic (then) Lieutenant Governor Patrick J. Lucey. His detailed account, based in part on information gained by patiently driving from county to county looking at ill-prepared donation lists, revealed that almost the entire corporate community bankrolled Republicans, who were able to outspend the Democrats 60–40 in most elections.

Among the few exceptions to this generality was Richard Cudahy, the young heir of a Milwaukee meat-packing fortune who joined the Democrats in 1964, became party chairman in 1967, and headed up Proxmire's re-election campaign in 1970. Cudahy adds to the respectability of the party in the eyes of the well-to-do, and is thought by party workers to be especially worthy because he can raise money in wealthy circles. Another prominent Democratic businessman who provides the exception to the rule is James Windham, president of Pabst Brewing, but Windham has Democratic roots that go back to his days as a middle-class Alabama youth just beginning his successful climb up the corporate ladder. After Cudahy and Windham, examples of business backing reach down to smaller businessmen like Catholic Francis Rondeau, a cheese processor who is probably not worth more than a million or two, and Jewish businessmen such as toymaker Jerry Colburn and plumbing supply contractor Bert Zion.

In Wisconsin, then, the liberals and an issue-oriented
electorate have bested a united and staunchly Republican
big-business community, but in order to do it they apparently had to have the leadership of an indefatigable patrician renegade with roots in Hill School, Yale, Harvard,
and J. P. Morgan & Co. William Proxmire is one of those
unexpected Democrats produced in small but consistent
quantities by the staid families of the upper crust.

WHAT WE LEARNED

Oscar and Andy Carr in Mississippi, Stephen and Audrey Currier of the Taconic Foundation, G. Mennen Williams in Michigan, William Proxmire in Wisconsin, and
Angier Biddle Duke and Jacob M. Kaplan of the National
Committee for an Effective Congress—these and the few
other Rolls-Royce liberals encountered in this chapter fall
in the patrician reform tradition of Franklin Roosevelt and
the New Deal. Their presence gives the governing circles
a degree of openness that makes small improvements possible at times by means of the electoral system. Limousine
liberals also reveal the potential of the Democratic Party
in a time of crisis. In a country where people's votes determine which clique of big rich will rule them, it is the
combination of enlightened patrician and aroused under
classes that is likely to win the day over paralyzed Republicans and pork-barrel Democrats.

At the same time, these establishment liberals who lead
the way to small social reforms also determine the left limit
of what is acceptable opinion within the American polity.
They use their wealth and prestige to encourage some
goals and strategies, and to discourage others. Their role
in discrediting the Progressive Party, in legitimizing the

Marshall Plan, in discouraging nonviolent direct action in the civil-rights movement, and in forcing loyal black Democrats to accept an unbalanaced compromise with segregationist Mississippi Democrats at the 1964 Democratic Convention are only the most dramatic examples of their continuous involvement in this limit-setting process. My interviews with journalists, scholars, and lawyers who have grown disenchanted with the limousine liberals they have observed at first-hand made it clear to me that more mundane examples of their centurion duties are equally abundant.

Because they play the sometimes-conflicting roles of both innovators and guardians, the establishment liberals are criticized from every angle. They are chastised by conservatives on the one hand for constantly trying to change certain aspects of the social system, harassed by radicals on the other for not being willing to work toward drastic social change. Only one thing is certain—the limousine liberals feel right at home within the contradictory confines of the Democratic Party.

5

THE MISRULING OF
AMERICA

Now that it is evident that the Democrats are hardly
the party of the common man, but rather the complex instrument of an odd assortment of successful Jewish businessmen, Irish politicos, conservative Southerners, and
maverick gentile patricians who sometimes work at cross-
purposes, the reader may feel misled and a bit let down
when I confess his trip through the financial minutiae
wasn't really necessary. It turns out political parties aren't
very important anymore, from a policy standpoint, so
who cares who rules the Democratic Party?

The weightiest authorities agree: crucial decisions are
made elsewhere, in the policy-formation process and the
special-interest process. American political parties aren't
much to brag about—they play their primary role in can-

didate selection. Of all the vital functions they could serve—political education, policy formulation, candidate selection, and social integration of regional and ethnic conflicts—they settle for just the latter two, culling out candidates and allowing us yet another national organization with which to overcome our ethnic and regional self-identities.

These revelations may come as a disappointment to those who believe campaign hoopla, political platforms, and the politicians on the TV screen are what it is all about. Saying parties aren't important borders on the treasonable. Therefore, to assuage any hard feelings, the next few pages will reveal the inside story of how the big policy decisions are made in America. Once this process is unveiled, the role of politics and political parties can be put in their proper (minor) place in the governmental process; then the foregoing chapters on the Democratic Party and its obese felines will be seen as worthwhile after all.

THE POLICY PROCESS

If political parties as they stand are so divorced from the decisions that misshape America, how in fact are various policies developed? The answer is in a little-known and seldom-studied sequence which begins in corporate board rooms and exclusive private clubs (where "issues" are identified as "problems" to be solved), moves to charitable foundations and special corporate discussion groups (where solutions to the problems are discussed), and winds up in the government (where the corporate solutions are adopted by executive order or congressional legislation).

Actually this corporation-to-discussion-group-to-government scheme as I have just presented it is slightly oversimplified. There is also in reality much movement back and forth of men and ideas from government to discussion group and from foundation to corporation. Then, too, middle-class career experts are injected into the scene at various points. The more complex reality can be studied in the accompanying diagram, where the aforementioned corporate discussion groups are labeled "consensus-seeking" and "policy-planning" organizations.

The handiest place to plunge into more detail about policy formation is with the consensus-seeking groups, for they are the Archimedean point in the whole process. These groups are made up of from several dozen to several hundred bankers, lawyers, and corporate executives from all over the country who meet together in small committees to discuss specific problems and to develop policy recommendations. It is in these cozy gatherings that powerful spokesmen representing all industries and all sections of the country seek consensus on problems of concern to the big-business community. The existence of these groups refutes any claim that the big rich are not politically organized, are not interested in political issues, or are not sophisticated about general problems of foreign and domestic policy.

FOREIGN POLICY

One of the most central of the power elite's consensus-seeking organs is the Council on Foreign Relations (at times abbreviated CFR hereafter). Organized by prominent businessmen and Wall Street lawyers shortly after

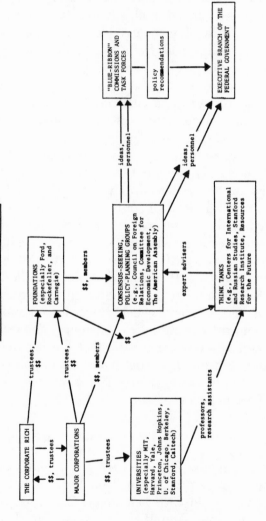

THE POWER ELITE POLICY-MAKING PROCESS

World War I, it was by World War II the heart of the clique which shapes foreign policy—regardless of which party is in power. It is a center from which many appointees to the State and Defense departments have been drawn, serving as a training ground for new leadership within the establishment.

The Council on Foreign Relations has several other functions. It sponsors a great amount of research with the money received from its friends at the Ford, Rockefeller, and Carnegie foundations. It publishes *Foreign Affairs,* the most prestigious journal in its field, as well as numerous other books and handbooks on world affairs. It has off-the-record meetings and luncheons where its New York members can hear talks by prominent Washington officials and foreign visitors. With money from the Carnegie Corporation, it sponsors Committees on Foreign Relations in thirty-four cities across the nation; the local businessmen, newspaper publishers, and university bigwigs comprising these committees are supplied with monthly lecturers who make it possible for the local opinion leaders to assume the role of informed experts on foreign policy when the need arises for them to make oracular public pronouncements.

For all its many functions, the most significant remains the small study groups of twenty to thirty men who meet weekly or monthly to discuss a particular problem. It is in these sessions that differences are ironed out and the opinions of experts are blended smoothly into the corporate mentality. A study group that met in the early fifties considered the possibility for social change within Russian society; in addition to anticommunist experts from Columbia and Harvard, the group included Averell Harriman, Dean Rusk, Devereaux Josephs (chairman of New

York Life Insurance, trustee of the Carnegie Corporation), Robert Amory of the CIA, and some lesser lights of
the power elite. A quiet seminar of the midfifties pondered
the problems of nuclear weapons; among its members
were such notables as Frank Altschul, McGeorge Bundy,
Thomas K. Finletter, Paul H. Nitze, and David Rockefeller. Out of this little gathering came Henry Kissinger's
Nuclear Weapons and Foreign Policy, a book that was
considered to be "a best seller which has been closely
read in the highest Administration circles and foreign
offices abroad." In the late fifties and early sixties study
groups reassessed U.S. policy toward Red China with the
help of a $900,000 grant from the Ford Foundation.

The Council on Foreign Relations and its committees
are not the whole of the foreign-policy establishment.
Closely associated with it in membership, financing, and
outlook is the Foreign Policy Association, an organization
which concentrates more on disseminating the gospel to
the "grass roots" of "attentive publics" within the upper
middle class and the academic community. And there are
other associations and institutes within the group, all
tightly interlocked in their leadership with CFR, the
Foreign Policy Association, and the corporations and
foundations which provide them with ample funds and
members. Perhaps it is enough to say that David Rockefeller, chairman of Chase Manhattan Bank and a trustee
of Rockefeller Brothers Fund, is the chairman of the Council on Foreign Relations and the Council for Latin America. But if it isn't, it could be added that as of 1970
ubiquitious Sol Linowitz of the Xerox Corporation, the
Council on Foreign Relations, the American Association
for the United Nations, the National Urban Coalition, and

the Institute of International Education was chairman of
the Foreign Policy Association, where seven of his ten
male vice-chairmen are also members of the Council on
Foreign Relations.*

The CFR–FPA foreign-policy establishment is not only
representative of the national power elite. It is neatly bipartisan, albeit tipped mildly to the Republican side. Some
of the biggest fat cats in both parties come together within
its august portals. Thus, 56 CFR members, including such
luminaries as United Artists' Robert Benjamin, IBM's
Thomas Watson, Lehman Brothers' John Lehman, and
Loeb, Rhoades' John L. Loeb, gave at least $265,000 to
the Democrats in 1968, while another 144 are on record for
$547,000 to the Republicans. Over at the Foreign Policy
Association, and here we are including 18 Democrats and
12 Republicans already counted at the Council on Foreign
Relations, 126 members of the National Council gave
$426,000 to Republicans, 71 gave $214,000 to Democrats.
Small wonder that CFR–FPA leaders are found to serve in
top strategic posts in both Republican and Democratic
administrations. Small wonder John F. Kennedy would
defer to Republican Robert A. Lovett of Brown Brothers,
Harriman in picking his key Defense and State department personnel. We can agree safely with establishment-
oriented journalist Joseph Kraft that "the Council plays a
special part in helping to bridge the gap between the two
parties, affording unofficially a measure of continuity
when the guard changes in Washington." And there is

* And if further evidence is needed, there is the detailed essay on "How
The Power Elite Make Foreign Policy" in my book *The Higher Circles*
(Random House, 1970).

no danger in agreeing with political scientist Dean Burnham, a reigning expert on political parties within the political science fraternity:

> . . . as is well known, in the United States the
> making of foreign-policy and military decisions is
> the province of a bipartisan elite drawn from the
> executive establishment and from private industry.
> It is not the province of the political parties, and
> it is not normally capable of being structured into
> a cluster of issues on which the parties are opposed
> and between which the voters can choose. Since
> these decisions involve the expenditure of between
> three-fifths and three-quarters of the current fed-
> eral administrative budget, depending upon which
> items are included, it is not inaccurate to say that
> most of the present-day activities of the federal
> government lie quite outside of areas in which par-
> ties can make any positive contributions to the po-
> litical system.

Burnham's well-considered views are consistent with
the theory that a power elite made up of millionaires and
their hired experts dominates the federal government, for
three fifths to three quarters of the national budget is not
a small piece of solid reality for any theory to encompass.
His suggestions almost completely contradict the ideas of
the sanguine collection of political scientists known as
"pluralists," who believe that many groups of Americans
—and not just the super-rich—are major factors in running the American government.

But there is more, for Burnham goes on to say that
"The non-partisan military-foreign affairs sector has come

more and more to infiltrate [sic!] the world of domestic politics and nominally domestic or private activities." Which in turn signifies there is "a growing restriction of the scope of effective party activity even here."

Thus, a leading student of political parties is on the verge of conceding domestic policy as well as foreign policy to the power elite. The next few paragraphs should suffice to make power-elite domination of the entire policy process all but official.

DOMESTIC POLICY

More and more people, then, are coming to believe that a power elite rooted in the assets of the big corporations and banks is the mover and shaker when it comes to foreign policy. But there are still some skeptics when it comes to domestic policy. They must be shown concretely how a network of corporate consensus-seeking organizations operate in the same way on domestic issues as do the Council on Foreign Relations and the Foreign Policy Association on foreign policy. Such a demonstration is possible, although only its major highlights will be presented here.*

The central policy-planning group in the case of domestic issues is the Committee for Economic Development (CED). Founded in 1942 by farsighted businessmen who feared another depression would develop after World War II if Keynesian-type economic policies were not adopted, the Committee for Economic Development consists of more than two hundred corporation leaders and (of late)

---

* Once again, the more complete picture (and a bibliography) can be found in *The Higher Circles*. Consult the essay on "How the Power Elite Shape Social Legislation."

a handful of university presidents. The members meet in small study groups with grant-laden economists from the intellectual establishment anchored at Harvard, Yale, Princeton, and the University of Chicago to hammer out position papers on various issues. They are ultra-generously funded by major foundations, and especially the Ford Foundation—a relationship that goes back to the time when one of CED's founders, Paul Hoffman of Studebaker Corporation, was also president of the Ford Foundation.

There is every indication that the Committee for Economic Development and its viewpoint are deferred to by the government. A case study of the Employment Act of 1946 shows that CED leaders played an indispensable conciliatory role between the liberals and the conservatives. Truman appointed a CED man, Republican Thomas McCabe (he gave $18,000 to Republicans in 1968), to head the Federal Reserve Board in 1948. Most of the top officials in the Marshall Plan were CED members. The Kennedy tax cut was recommended and pushed by the CED. The reorganized budget system put in operation in 1969 reads much like the CED plan; and one of Nixon's staff economic advisers, Herb Stein, was for years the chief economic consultant for CED. And so on.

Like the Council on Foreign Relations and the Foreign Policy Association, the CED is bipartisan. However, because of its intentional de-emphasis of Wall Street lawyers and investment bankers, it is dominated by middle-ground Republicans. While ninety-five members were giving at least $309,000 to Republicans in 1968, only sixteen of its members were on record as giving $61,000 to Democrats. Along with such main-line fat cats as Edgar B. Stern, Jr., of New Orleans, Ed Pauley of Los Angeles, and Philip Klutznick of Chicago, the Democrats in CED include two well-known liberals, Robert Nathan of the Americans for Democratic Action and William Benton of the Encyclopaedia Britannica.*

The Committee for Economic Development is careful not to lobby, but its members know how to put its non-political and bipartisan images to good political use. One of the best examples of this occurred in May, 1970, when several CED leaders came to San Francisco to chat with other big businessmen in support of Nixon's new minimal yearly income plan at a special one-day "policy forum." The mission was especially significant because California's ultra-slick right-wing Governor, former actor Ronald Reagan, was against the plan. In addition to private conversations with high-placed people, the CED visitors held a press conference designed to put public pressure on the Governor.

A local CED leader, S. Clark Beise, former president of the Bank of America, spoke first to the reporters, noting that "this whole subject was studied carefully by our CED members, who are businessmen, and who consulted with the experts." So two crushing influences on American opinion—businessmen and experts—were invoked by Beise. Then a Democrat, oilman George McGhee of Texas, who served as Kennedy's ambassador to West Germany, put in the bipartisan pitch: "Lots of Democrats agree with this program." McGhee's remarks were followed by a question concerning Reagan's opposition, which was an-

* When Citizens' Research Foundation published the list of 1968 donors of $500 or more, Benton wrote to the foundation to let them know that he had given not $12,500, but $50,000. He then wondered if other people's donations were similarly understated. Given the problems of compiling accurate lists, they probably were.

swered in tasteful style by another visiting fireman, Samuel J. Silberman of New York.

After gently chiding Reagan as a "sore winner," Silberman said: "I've had a chance to read some of your Governor's stuff, and his statements say his objections stem from 'philosophical antipathy.' I think these very words say that his is not an objective, logical point of view." The CED man clearly had Reagan out on a philosophical limb, which is hardly a good one to be on in "pragmatic" America, while he himself took the solid scientific ground of objectivity and good sense. All in all, the press conference was a virtuoso performance by the CED, and one that is regularly repeated around the country on a variety of issues deemed suitable for the CED program of one-day policy forums.

As with the Council on Foreign Relations and the Foreign Policy Association on foreign policy, the Committee for Economic Development is simply the best known and most important of several power-elite organizations that supplement it and orbit around it—organizations such as The Brookings Institution, the National Bureau for Economic Research (which was forced by the Ford Foundation in 1967 to move further into the mainstream or lose financial support), the American Assembly, and the National Planning Association. These enterprises develop mildly reasonable solutions to social problems and then create, through books, pamphlets, speeches, news releases, and discussion groups, the grass-roots support that is often needed to induce Congress to adopt them. They also prepare their members and employees for government service as department heads, presidential advisers, and congressional consultants.

It should come as no great surprise that the same peo-

ple who run the CFR and the Foreign Policy Association
are the leaders of the organizations that shape domestic
policies. They are the same people not only in the sense of
being rich bankers, lawyers, and corporate leaders who
are friends, neighbors, and clubmates, but also in the lit-
eral sense of being one and the same individuals. Thus,
51 of 284 Committee for Economic Development trustees
and honorary trustees were in 1968 members of the Council on Foreign Relations, and 26 were members of the
National Council of the Foreign Policy Association.
Eleven key men, including such prominent Democrats as
Stanley Marcus of Neiman-Marcus, Robert Nathan of
ADA, and William M. Roth of San Francisco's Matson
Navigation Company, were ensconced in all three organizations. Dean Burnham probably knows how right-on-tar-
get he is in quietly suggesting to his cautious political
science colleagues that the "non-partisan military-foreign
affairs sector" has "infiltrated" the "world of domestic
politics."

So, to repeat with emphasis, the political parties are not
centers for policy making, and that includes domestic policy as well as foreign policy. Policy formation is the
province of a bipartisan power elite of corporate rich and
their career hirelings who work through an interlocking
and overlapping maze of foundations, universities, institutes, discussion groups, associations, and commissions.
Political parties are only for finding interesting and genial
people (usually ambitious middle-class lawyers) to ratify
and implement these policies in such a way that the under
classes feel themselves to be, somehow, a part of the governmental process. Politics is not exactly the heart of the
action, but it is nice work—if you can afford to campaign
for it.

THE DINOSAUR CLUB

The foregoing makes it sound too easy to put a policy into practice. Everyone can see by the newspapers that there is in America struggle, delay, and compromise over a wide range of both foreign and domestic issues. The reason for this struggle, oddly enough, is not usually attributable to large-scale opposition from any of the under classes, which are variously numb, bedazzled, and wildly misinformed. It stems more often from disagreements within the power elite. The more conservative elements of the well-to-do, and there are a significant number of them, do not go along with many of the policies of the CFR–FPA–CED axis. They are for older-fashioned, belt-tightening, head-knocking kinds of solutions to problems —like total victories overseas and rising unemployment at home. Some of the wilder members of this group appear to believe David Rockefeller and his wealthy compatriots are communists in disguise only waiting for the right moment to sell out the United States to the Reds of Moscow and the Pinks of London. They have held this belief for about thirty-five years now, despite considerable evidence to the contrary.

Politically speaking, these ultra-conservatives are the right-wing Republicans and the conservative Southern Democrats. They have their own apparatchiki of tax-exempt foundations, trade associations, journals, and pressure groups which grind out an unending stream of blood-curdling pamphlets, films, records, speeches, and position papers pushing the right-wing line. At the heart of this sprawling network, which literally dwarfs the little liberal clique outlined in the previous chapter, is the National Association of Manufacturers (abbreviated NAM), a nationwide trade association that has been in the rearguard of every issue since its members declared war on organized labor in 1902. It is the laughingstock of any halfway literate American, but it has been quite effective in emasculating progressive legislation of even the mildest variety.

Working closely with the National Association of Manufacturers, and just as important and backward looking, are the U.S. Chamber of Commerce, the American Farm Bureau Federation (which has as many hard-right business leaders as it has corporate farmers and plantation owners), and the National Cotton Council. These organizations, unlike the Council on Foreign Relations and the Committee for Economic Development, function as pressure groups and lobbies as well as engage in policy formation and public relations. They look out for the day-to-day interests of various corporations on specific issues, while CFR and CED tend to concentrate on the more general direction of the corporate system. They are complemented by satellite foundations and front groups such as the Tax Foundation, the Farm Foundation, the Foundation for Economic Education, the American Enterprise Association, the American Security Council, the National Industrial Conference Board, the Southern States Industrial Council, a myriad of single-industry trade associations, and local chambers of commerce. Also operating in this system, and deriving considerable protection from it, is the American Medical Association.

It is these organizations and their corporate leaders which fuel the conservative coalition in Congress, often using small-town hicks and gullible hayseeds as their "rural" front. Not content with innumerable organizational interlocks and the utilization of the same gaggle of speakers at official meetings of the various groups, they even gather secretly each year for their Greenbrier Conference in the resort town of White Sulphur Springs, West Virginia, to map out their lobbying strategy for the coming year—a fact which didn't make an impression in social-science circles until nineteen years after the Greenbrier Conferences were inaugurated in 1950.* In addition to lobbying, the groups of the conservative bloc also help ultra-conservative Congressmen by sending news releases and editorials to small-town and rural newspapers, by encouraging local chambers of commerce to lean on their Congressmen, and by underwriting right-wing Republicans and conservative (usually Southern) Democrats in congressional elections.

The major differences between the sophisticated conservatives of the CFR-CED and the simple-minded conservatives of the NAM circles, which have been recognizable for a long time, were drawn out in more detail in studies of both groups in the late fifties and early sixties. Committee for Economic Development members tend to be more internationally minded in foreign affairs, supporting foreign aid and lower tariffs, while the National Association of Manufacturer types as a group are more hostile to foreign aid and favor higher tariffs. The differences between the two orientations within the power elite are

---

* Needless to say, no member of the academic community has bestirred himself to study other than one or another narrow aspect of the ultra-conservative half of the power elite. The best study of it remains journalist Wesley McCune's *Who's Behind Our Farm Policy?* (Frederick A. Praeger, Inc., 1956), which explores the reactionaries from the angle of their malevolent involvement in the ongoing destruction of the small farmer.

even greater on domestic policy: the CFR–CED mentality supports—nay, developed—the policies of the welfare state in order to increase consumer spending and fend off more serious social change, but this farsightedness is lost on the NAM mentality, which was against Social Security, the recognition of organized labor, and Medicare when these measures were first introduced.

One of the most interesting public exchanges between CED and NAM took place over a CED-financed statement on collective bargaining and the American economy. In 1959 the CED commissioned several leading experts on labor-management relations to compose an independent report. Even though it expressly was not a policy statemet of the CED, it incurred the wrath of the NAM and its cohorts when it appeared in 1962 for suggesting that anti-union "right-to-work" laws be abolished. Several financial contributors to the CED even withdrew their support. One distraught corporate leader charged that the CED was being run by its staff—not the trustees—and that this dangerous, perhaps subversive staff was using the money and prestige provided by the CED to injure "the interests of the very ones supplying the money for the effort—as well as progressively impairing the whole free-market, private property, limited government arrangement under which we have been able to have and enjoy freedom."

The leader of the sneaky staff in question was George P. Shultz, a professor at the University of Chicago who serves in the Nixon Administration as director of a key control center, the Office of Management and Budget. The perverse committee for which he labored was headed by economist Clark Kerr, then president of the University of California, and it included economists, political scientists, and labor-relations experts from Harvard, MIT, Brown, and the University of Chicago.

Taken aback, the Committee for Economic Development, which after all likes right-to-work laws because they hinder union growth, tried to explain that it had purposely decided to "live dangerously" in order to obtain an independent view. It then appointed its own blue-ribbon study group to prepare an official CED policy statement on labor unions. Serving on this Labor Policy Subcommittee, among others, were the chairmen of American Can, U.S. Steel, Montgomery Ward, Alcoa, and Scott Paper, all nonsubversives. The report, published in 1964, was endorsed by the Research and Policy Committee as a whole, a group including chieftains from Bank of America, Standard Oil of New Jersey, Merck & Co., AT&T, Federated Department Stores, Ford Motor, and Dun & Bradstreet. As the historian employed by CED to tell its story has written, the labor report fashioned by the board chairmen was "not one of CED's happiest productions." Among other things, the new formulation endorsed right-to-work laws and blamed unions for contributing to inflation. Relations with the National Association of Manufacturers now improved considerably.

Where, then, do CED and NAM differ on labor policy? Well, CED would allow unions to exist, although in a weaker condition than they are even now. The National Association of Manufacturers would like to smash them. The difference between CED and NAM in their attitude toward trade unions also can be seen in the fact that the NAM types would no more risk letting mere academics write an independent report for them on this delicate topic than they would consider having the Communist

Politburo write one. The difference is a subtle one, not always given to differences in practice, but it is a difference. Around Washington they explain it by saying NAM operates with a sledgehammer, whereas CED prefers the scalpel.

It is sometimes said that the conservative clique reflects the outlook of smaller and local businesses. This is partly true and partly not true. It is true that the NAM, which is above all a trade association, has among its members many "smaller" big businessmen whose businesses are not in the top few hundred corporations, and that the U.S. Chamber of Commerce has to keep in touch with the petty millionaires of small towns and rural areas. However, it is also true that these organizations are bossed and financed by men who are in many cases just as wealthy and powerful as those who run the CED. If these men were to withdraw their support, as they sometimes do on foreign-policy matters, the old-fashioned conservatives wouldn't have a chance against the CFR–CED juggernaut, which has labor unions and middle-class liberals behind it on any halfway reasonable program it wishes to put forth.

Two of the most obvious examples of these arch-conservatives are the du Ponts and the Pews. The du Ponts are among the wealthiest extended families in America, and their corporations are both big and international, but most members of the family have been ultra-reactionary. In 1946, for example, when the conservatives were too demoralized to fight the Employment Act, it was a member of the du Pont group who used the NAM as a front to stir up considerable opposition to the bill and force several changes in it, just as in 1936 it was the du Ponts and other big stockholders in General Motors who funded the

Liberty League in its ill-tempered campaign against Roosevelt. Today, few du Ponts are found within the ranks of CFR and CED, but they gave money to Goldwater, support the NAM, and run a chain of right-wing suburban newspapers. There need be no hesitation in naming the Wilmington clan as the Number One Enemy of middle-of-the-road accommodation in the United States.*

Closely behind the du Ponts in their retarding influence are the Pews, who own and manage Sun Oil, one of the fifty largest industrial companies in the country. Not only do they finance right-wing Republicans and support conservative policies within the NAM, among crackpot affiliations too numerous to mention, but they have a considerable influence within agribusiness through their ownership of the *Farm Journal,* one of the largest farm magazines in the country.

There are many other families and their companies that could be singled out, but the du Ponts and Pews make the point as well as any other ten such groups. It is not enough, then, to say that the conservative coalition represents smaller, less international businesses, for it is energized by a group of ultra-conservative families of great wealth who fit every stereotype ever invented to describe the grasping, greedy, narrow-minded, self-seeking robber baron. Without them the right wing would be a hollow and futile voice on the American scene.

Perhaps I have overdrawn the differences between the conservatives and the reactionaries within the power elite. It must be remembered that the families of both groups intermarry (a Roosevelt even married a du Pont and the

---

* With apologies to Mrs. James Faulkner of Brookline, Massachusetts, —a du Pont who gave $25,000 to Eugene McCarthy in 1968.

offspring is a strong liberal), go to the same schools, belong to the same clubs, and even sit on some of the same corporate boards. They share many more agreements than they evidence disagreements. This is particularly clear in two of the most important areas of concern to them—foreign policy, where many of those of the National Association of Manufacturer mentality go along with the notion of at least some foreign aid, and labor policy, where both can agree to endorse right-to-work laws and do everything they can, in their own separate ways, to keep organized labor on the defensive. Many of their differences, moreover, are questions of degree, and are within a shared context of profit-seeking and tax avoidance that is of much more importance to them than most political issues.

Nor are CED and NAM members without considerable contact in policy-formulating groups. One of the most important meeting grounds in this respect is the Business Council, a select group of business leaders who gather quietly three or four times a year at Hot Springs, Virginia, to confer with government officials. Most of what goes on at these meetings is off the record, but the corporate czars do make an occasional pronouncement which indicates their degree of satisfaction with how the politicos are minding the corporate outposts in Washington. These pronouncements, and any attendant suggestions, often reflect a sort of CED–NAM compromise on what the government should do about a given problem.

So the CED and NAM mentalities are not black and white. Furthermore, there is reason to believe that the CED is winning its ideological struggle with the NAM. The CED clearly has the NAM on the defensive, and the NAM is bowing to more CED positions every day. Stories appeared several times during the sixties extolling the

"new image" and the "new leadership" at the National
Association of Manufacturers, which in any case overlaps
in membership with the Committee for Economic Development.

THE POLICY STRUGGLE

Now that the highly conservative coalition rooted in
the National Association of Manufacturers has been outlined, the policy struggle can be understood in all its
complexity. There are three groupings which fight over
policy in Washington. The first is the liberal-labor coalition outlined in the previous chapter. The second is the
CFR–CED clique which dominates the centrist wings of
both political parties, and the third is the rightist coalition rooted in the NAM, U.S. Chamber of Commerce,
American Farm Bureau, and National Cotton Council.
The major strength of the sophisticated conservatives of
the Committee for Economic Development variety is in the
executive branch, the major strength of the reactionary
conservatives is in Congress, and the liberals do not have
any major strength. When push comes to shove, the liberals are forced to hope that the CFR–CED group will be
on their side. Otherwise, they are trampled.

In fact, the leanings of the CFR–CED faction go a long
way toward determining the outcome of any policy struggle. If the CFR–CED group decides to go in the direction
of change, it develops a plan, or modifies a plan already
developed by rich liberals, and then enlists the support of
liberals, organized labor, and the National Farmers
Union. If the CFR–CED group decides there is no need
for change, which means that the two most powerful
groups within the power elite are united, it sits by silently

while the conservative forces unmercifully bludgeon any suggestions put forth by labor or liberals.

The liberals, then, are helpless without the support of the sophisticated conservatives within the power elite. The ultra-rightists, however, are not helpless without the support of their more restrained brethren. They do not roll over and play dead just because the CFR–CED fence-sitters are on the other side of the field. Due to the ultra-conservatives' strength within Congress, there are no easy victories for the ameliorists when they go against the right anchor of the power elite.

It may even be that the outcome of a conservative-versus-reactionary battle within the power elite depends upon who is in the White House, for the sophisticated elements seem to do better when there is a Democratic President. Kennedy, for instance, gave them just about everything they wanted, and Johnson gave them even more. A Nixon, on the other hand, sitting precariously on the CED–NAM fault line within the Republican Party, is often too shackled to the ultra-conservative Republicans to swing his weight fully on the side of the sophisticated conservatives.

COMMON CAUSE

More research needs to be done on the ways in which the sophisticated conservatives and the reactionaries ply their trade in Congress. However, it seems likely that John Gardner's Common Cause is a symptom of the failure of the CFR–CED axis to do all it would like within that bastion of senility and delay. John Gardner is the former president of the Carnegie Corporation, which is certainly one of the linchpins in the mildly enlightened faction of the power elite. In 1965 Republican Gardner was appointed by Democrat Johnson to be the Secretary of Health, Education, and Welfare. After a three-year tour of duty, Gardner departed government service right at the time when the ghetto uprisings were causing consternation in the big-business community. He was soon tapped by his well-heeled friends to head a new consensus-seeking organization, the National Urban Coalition, which would include blacks, labor leaders, and local government officials as well as the usual corporate dukes from the Council on Foreign Relations and the Committee for Economic Development. The Urban Coalition did a lot of talking, and wrote up some polite position papers, but it accomplished very little of substance.

Hampered in lobbying efforts by the tax-exempt status of the National Urban Coalition, and feeling the need for more grass roots support from the general citizenry, Gardner and a few wealthy backers took the "action arm" of the National Urban Coalition out of the organization in early 1970 and transformed it into an independent entity, Common Cause.* It was funded at the outset—"seed money"—by Eugene McCarthy backer Howard Stein on the left and moderate Republican John D. Rockefeller, III, on the right, with Democratic fat cats Sol Linowitz and Arthur Krim and Republican heavyweights Norton Simon and John Hay Whitney chipping in from the center.

Faced with this powerful leadership competition from the financial pinnacles, various liberal groups, including millionaire Harold Willen's Businessmen's Education Fund, soon fell into step behind Common Cause. A mem-

---

* However, Common Cause remained in its plush offices in the Washington building rented by the National Urban Coalition.

bership drive was started in order to enlist the average
American, meaning anyone willing to pay a yearly membership fee of $15. Full-page ads were taken out in Sun-
day newspapers and political magazines, while letters
were sent to everyone whose name had ever been affixed
to one of dozens of liberal and moderate mailing lists.*
Then a Policy Council was set up—including such luminaries as Andrew Heiskell, chairman of Time, Inc., and an
original cochairman of the Urban Coalition, W. D. Eberle,
president of American Standard, Inc., and a contributor
of $5,500 to Republican candidates in 1968, Richard
Hatcher, the black mayor of Gary, Indiana, John V. Lind-
say, the WASP mayor of New York, John Wheeler, president of the Southern Regional Council, and various other
businessmen, educators, religious leaders, and prominent
minority spokesmen. Common Cause was ready for action.

Now, Common Cause is backing many desperately-
needed actions, like peace and putting the country back
together, but for our purposes it is essential to realize
how eager Common Cause claims to be about making
changes in Congress. That is, it is for reducing the power
of the conservative coalition in Congress. It wants to make
the Congress more "responsive," which probably means the
Carnegie Corporation people and the Rockefellers have
come to agree with the limousine liberals that there must
be more in the way of palliative social welfare, urban re-
clamation, and civil rights.

Common Cause may be a signal that the centrist rich
have decided for the first time to join with the liberal National Committee for an Effective Congress in trying to
bring change to the citadel of the NAM-rural mentality,
although it is possible that they would be willing to live

* People claim to have received the same letter up to fourteen times.

and let live again if the Vietnam war were to end or discontent were to be guided to manageable levels by the
usual subterfuges and threats. Whichever way the Common Cause crowd may go in the future, and whatever
the outcome of any internal struggle within the power
elite over Congress, it is clear that the political parties are
not formulating the issues or developing the policies of
the confrontation. As the experts warned us, the parties
just aren't that important.

THE SPECIAL INTEREST PROCESS

The foregoing scrutiny of the policy-making process
concerns the ways in which general issues are formulated
and resolved. But everything of importance to the upper
crust does not involve general issues. There are also a
great many specific policies and rulings made by government personnel which are of concern to specific industries
or individual corporations. The power elite have developed ways of taking care of these problems—ways which
also bypass the political parties and the campaign process.
We can call these various devices the special-interest process, and here we are talking about the quiet channels
through which the corporate rich get special favors or specific rulings for particular industries or corporations.

The prime method for gaining special favors is lobbying. This is first of all conducted by corporation lawyers,
who were shown in the first chapter to be willing servants
of both Democratic and Republican fat cats whatever
their own personal political persuasions. Their lobbying is
often at a lofty and subtle level, and there is sometimes
the claim that it isn't even lobbying. Lobbying is also done
by men hired by specific industries or corporations. It is

here that the National Association of Manufacturers and other trade associations are at their most effective. Sometimes the lobbyists are ex-politicos who, though defeated in an election, want to stay in Washington. They draw on their own legislative experience and friendships with elected and appointed officials of both parties to give their employers "access" to the committee of Congress or the particular department of the executive branch which can grant a special tax favor or procedural ruling.

Political lines are of course readily crossed when lobbyists are hired. The Republican du Ponts are able to hire a Democrat to do their lobbying, and the soft-voiced Republicans of Kuhn, Loeb can hire an Alabama friend of Democratic Senator John Sparkman of the Banking Committee when their CIT Financial Corporation needs a special clause in a bill so that it will be allowed to devour another large bank. Needless to say, lobbyists reciprocate any favors by providing a large but unknown percentage of the campaign funds that help keep favor givers of both parties in office; the special-interest crew is strictly nonpartisan in its beneficences.

There are other ways that corporate leaders can thank those who see things their way. For example, they use the Congressman's own public-relations firm, or they hire him to speak on ceremonial occasions for high fees. One of the most-used gambits is to pay a fat retainer fee to his law firm back in the home district. The late Drew Pearson and Jack Anderson did a quick check of fifty "typical" law firms that have partners serving in Congress. They found that "Some of the biggest corporate names in America are listed as clients of Congressmen's law firms in such out of the way places, say, as Nicholasville, Kentucky, and Pascagoula, Mississippi." Literally no persuasive stone is left unturned by those practicing within the special-interest sphere, and this of course includes the old standbys —liquor, junkets, and lissome women.

Corporate lawyers concentrate much of their attention on regulatory agencies; ordinary lobbyists tend to concentrate on Congress. To assure proper behavior from the executive branch, the power elite supplement lawyers and lobbyists through specially-appointed committees whose members are drawn from the corporate community. These government-sanctioned committees monitor every important activity of the departments and agencies of the federal executive. Some, like the committee on oil, dictate much of the policy developed by the department that concerns them; others merely hamper and sidetrack the execution of public-interest policies having to do with pollution, consumer protection, and industrial safety. The Advisory Council on Federal Reports, an industry-funded octopus of committees and subcommittees that criticizes federal reports for the Budget Bureau, delayed implementation of one antipollution measure for seven years. The subcommittee representing the automotive industry rendered innocuous a questionnaire the National Highway Safety Bureau wanted to send out in order to find out more about auto-repair problems.

Such little horror stories could continue through a maze of over three thousand committees, commissions, and boards. This vast network is an "invisible bureaucracy" of big businessmen which oversees and advises on the functioning of the government, making sure that coal mines are not inspected, that drug and food companies are not properly regulated, and that cattlemen are allowed to do as they will while grazing their herds on public lands. The special advisory committees of the executive branch are among the least-known and most powerful means by which specific industries guard their narrow interest against the general welfare.

THE PARTIES ONCE AGAIN

The policy process and the special-interest process are obviously far more crucial than the political parties in the ruling of America, especially when we think of politics in terms of *who gets what*—that is, in terms of the distribution of wealth and other widely coveted rewards. However, the policy process and the special-interest process could not operate as unfairly and corruptly as they do if the campaigns did not produce elected officials willing to acquiesce in large-scale pilferage by the power elite in exchange for tenuous "power," phony glory, and the chance to make a lot of money for themselves if they play their cards deftly.

Thus, the super-rich who are our rulers concern themselves with politics so that the proper kinds of candidates will be selected. The campaign process does have its place in the decisions that distort America. What Democratic and Republican fat cats try to do within their respective parties is insure the nomination of properly moderate and pliable candidates; the unchanging pattern of the wealth distribution suggests that they have done a good job.

Nevertheless, the candidate-selection process is not absolutely rigged. Sometimes a ringer slips through in one party or the other: Democratic and Republican fund raisers working alone within their respective parties are sometimes temporarily outfoxed by other groups or individuals who put forth an energetic candidate. It then becomes necessary for like-minded fat cats of both parties to work together in isolating unacceptable candidates. Of recent decades these undesirables usually have been overly conservative Republicans. The most dramatic example was in 1964 when a great many super-wealthy middle-of-the-road Republicans either defected to Johnson or gave less than their usual amount of financial support to the Republicans.

Although most power-elite problems have involved right-wingers, there are times when liberals must be put in their place decisively by the combined efforts of the corporate brotherhood. A recent example of ganging up on liberals occurred in the state of Washington in 1970. The liberal, antiwar Democrats announced they were going to challenge their hawkish Democratic Senator, Henry Jackson, in the Democratic primary. Fearful that this faithful friend of Boeing Aircraft might be hurt by this dissension within his party, two of the wealthiest Republicans in the state hastily formed a committee to raise bipartisan money for his re-election campaign. One was William Allen, head of Boeing Aircraft, the other was William Reed, owner of Simpson Timber, one of the largest privately held businesses in the country. They had little trouble tapping millionaires at Seattle's Rainier Club and other wealth-laden mansions around the state and nation. Jackson not only won the primary, but went on to a smashing victory in the regular election against a patsy who got little support from the GOP money cats who were too busy rooting for Jackson.

The lackadaisical Republican effort against Jackson in the regular election in 1970 reveals another way the wealthy of both parties cooperate—sometimes they just don't run very hard against their friends in the other party. No checkbook Democrat in New York would lend a nickel to an effort to unseat Republican Senator Jacob Javits, nor would any of the Republican fat cats in Chicago dig up big money to oppose their favorite benefactor, Democratic Mayor Richard Daley.

All these special campaign bargains between large Republican and Democratic donors work to one purpose—they tend to isolate liberal Democrats and reactionary Republicans. More generally, politics is kept issueless; the promise of political education is ignored by campaigns, which remain exercises in image building, paranoia, name-calling, and gossip-mongering. The fat cats want the political parties to produce ambitious exhibitionists willing to adopt as their own the pronouncements and policies the bipartisan power elite develops through its foundations, institutes, associations, and special committees.

AND FINALLY THE END

Well, there you have it. The policy-making process is in the hands of the grasping rich, whether of a halfway humane or a reactionary hue, and the political parties are mortgaged to favor-seeking fat cats who want to keep campaigns as trivial personality contests. Even the Democratic Party, the wondrous political organization sometimes unjustly celebrated as the party of the common man, is little more than an unending series of broken promises. To say that it is the best Americans can do any time soon, as ADA liberal John Kenneth Galbraith is probably accurate in assuring us, is hardly encouraging, for that means wealth and income will remain concentrated to an incredible degree in the hands of the very rich, the tax system will remain regressive and unfair to the struggling wage earner, and the costs of an anemic welfare state will rest on the shoulders of middle Americans.

It is not a pretty picture, but it is inevitable as long as the under classes find no difficulty in pinning their hopes on a party containing both fat cats and plain democrats. Until the unlikely day when millions of blue- and white-collar workers put aside their racial and ethnic differences and show themselves to be genuine democrats by contributing $10 to $20 a year to the support of anti-Big Property candidates, American politics will remain with few exceptions a staging area for blustery egotists, timid idealists, and the usual array of favor seekers, tax dodgers, and outright embezzlers. The essence of power elite politics is bamboozlement, and no group should be disappointed to find itself continually left out in the cold by sweet-talking Democrats who are bought and paid for by the big rich.

BIBLIOGRAPHIC ESSAY

This brief bibliographic essay is only intended to inform the reader of basic reference sources on campaign finance and the Democratic Party. It is not meant to be exhaustive, for I drew from many books, journals, magazines, newspapers, and interviews in addition to the original research carried out with the aid of research assistants in developing my analysis of the Democratic Party.

This essay also serves to identify the sources for quotations which did not come from interviews or minor newspaper articles.

CHAPTER 1: ONE BIG PROPERTY PARTY

For general information on campaign finance, see Alexander Heard, *The Costs of Democracy* (Doubleday &

Co., 1962) and Herbert E. Alexander, *Financing the 1968 Election* (D. C. Heath and Company, 1971). These two books contain many useful references as well as original information. Several short studies published by the Citizens' Research Foundation, 245 Nassau Street, Princeton, New Jersey, also are excellent sources for gaining an overall picture of campaign finance.

Recent information on the motives of fat cats, and on the various methods by which political money is quietly passed from wealthy men to candidates is presented in "The Politician as an Investment," a chapter from the book by Morton Mintz and Jerry S. Cohen, *America, Inc.* (Dial Press, 1971). For background material on party supporters and the political attitudes of American voters, I am indebted to Richard Hamilton, *Class and Politics in the United States* (John Wiley & Sons, 1971). Unlike *Fat Cats and Democrats*, Hamilton's book has a comprehensive bibliography covering the relevant publications of sociologists, political scientists, and historians, and it should be consulted by those seeking detailed information on all aspects of American politics.

The quotation from Dean Acheson on pages 16–17 can be found in William A. Williams, *The Contours of American History* (World Publishing Company, 1961, pages 371–72). The comment immediately following from Averell Harriman is on page 8 of the *NACLA Newsletter*, Vol. II, No. 8 (December, 1968); it originally appeared in *The New York Times Magazine* (March 5, 1967). The quote from Ferdinand Lundberg which appears on page 26 is from his *The Rich and The Super-Rich* (Lyle Stuart, 1968, page 41).

A down-to-earth account of the Founding Fathers and their financial concerns in writing the Constitution can be found in Chapter Two of Thomas R. Dye and L. Harmon

Zeigler, *The Irony of Democracy* (Wadsworth Publishing Company, 1970).

The financing of party conventions is spelled out in John F. Bibby and Herbert E. Alexander, *The Politics of National Convention Finances and Arrangements* (Study Number 14, Citizens' Research Foundation, 245 Nassau Street, Princeton, New Jersey). The quote on page 29 is from page 64 of the Bibby-Alexander study.

For information on organized labor and politics, see Harry M. Scoble, "Organized Labor in Electoral Politics: Some Questions for the Discipline," *Western Political Quarterly* (1963), pages 666–85 and J. David Greenstone, *Labor in American Politics* (Alfred A. Knopf, 1969). Also informative about labor financial contributions in one state is John P. White and John R. Owens, *Parties, Group Interests and Campaign Finance: Michigan '56* (Study Number 2, Citizens' Research Foundation), which shows that the financial role of organized labor in the Democratic Party is exaggerated even in that highly-unionized state. The statement by Senator Russell Long, in the footnote on page 32, is conveniently found in Lundberg's previously-cited *The Rich and The Super-Rich*, page 717, or Mintz and Cohen's *America, Inc.*, page 158.

For evidence concerning organized labor's collaboration with the CIA, see my *The Higher Circles* (Random House, 1970, pages 261–65) and Dan Kurzman, "Lovestone's Cold War—The AFL-CIO Has Its Own CIA," *The New Republic* (June 25, 1966).

For support of the claim that the upper one and one-half percent of the wealthholders in fact receive twenty-four percent of the nation's yearly income, which is higher than some scholars claim, see the arguments and evidence of economist James D. Smith, "An Estimate of the Income of the Very Rich," *Papers in Quantitative Economics* (University Press of Kansas, 1968).

CHAPTER 2: JEWS AND COWBOYS

For general information on the Jewish investment bankers, see Vincent P. Carosso, *Investment Banking in America: A History* (Harvard University Press, 1970); Allan Nevins, *Herbert Lehman and His Era* (Charles Scribner's Sons, 1963); E. Digby Baltzell, *The Protestant Establishment* (Random House, 1964); Barry E. Supple, "A Business Elite: German-Jewish Financiers in Nineteenth-Century New York," *Business History Review*, Vol. 31, No. 2; Stephen Birmingham, *Our Crowd* (Harper & Row, 1967); and three excellent articles by T. A. Wise, "The Bustling House of Lehman," *Fortune* (December, 1957); "Wherever You Look, There's Loeb, Rhoades," *Fortune* (April, 1963); and "Lazard: In Trinity There Is Strength," *Fortune* (August, 1968). The quotations from Wise which begin this chapter are from the opening sentences of his 1968 article on Lazard Freres.

The distinction between Yankees and Jews within the investment banking community is drawn from Carosso's just-mentioned book on the history of investment banking. A polarity between "Yankees" (meaning Northern big businessmen of Anglo-Saxon origins) and "Cowboys" was first suggested to me in personal conversations with Carl Ogelsby. His ideas on this polarity are partially developed in his column "Contradictions" in *Ramparts* (October and November, 1971). What I did, in effect, was empirically link Carosso's Jewish investment bankers with Ogelsby's Cowboys and contrast them with the old-line Republican gentiles who predominate in the corporate community.

The classic statement on interest groups, including a good discussion of the difficult problems in establishing their exact boundaries, is by Paul Sweezy, "Interest Groups in the American Economy," first published in 1939, and reprinted in his *The Present as History* (Monthly Review Press, 1953). For recent empirical material on interest groups, material which may not be accurate in many of its details, see Victor Perlo, *The Empire of High Finance* (International Publishers, 1957) and S. Menshikov, *Millionaires and Managers* (Progress Publishers, 1969).

My assertion of a Jewish-Cowboy interest group is based upon familial ties, common stock ownerhip, interlocking directorships, and common investment bankers. In addition to the references noted in the first paragraph of this section, I worked from articles on the investment banking firms in *The New York Times* over the past forty years and from articles in magazines indexed in *Readers' Guide to Periodical Literature* over the same time span. Mixed results concerning the existence of such an interest group came out of several interviews on this subject.

On Jews in American politics, see Lawrence Fuchs, *The Political Behavior of American Jews* (The Free Press, 1956); Ferdinand Lundberg, *America's Sixty Families* (Vanguard Press, 1937); and E. Digby Baltzell, *The Protestant Establishment* (Random House, 1964). Pages 423–28 of Alexander Heard's aforementioned *The Costs of Democracy* also contain interesting information on this subject.

The quotation on page 64 from Democratic adviser Sidney Hyman appears in Douglass Cater, *Power in Washington* (Random House, 1965, page 181).

On corporate lawyers and politics, see Andrew Kopkind and James Ridgeway, "Law and Power in Washington,"

Hard Times (June 16–23, 1969); Sheldon Zalaznick, "The Small World of Washington Lawyers," *Fortune* (September, 1969); and Drew Pearson and Jack Anderson, *The Case Against Congress* (Simon and Schuster, 1968). The information on O'Melveny and Myers lawyers close to both Democrats and Republicans in California appeared in George Murphy, "LA Law Firm: Services to Both Parties," San Francisco *Chronicle* (May 24, 1970), page 4.

CHAPTER 3: THE SOUTHERN ALBATROSS

For an understanding of the overall picture in Southern politics, see Dewey Grantham, Jr., *The Democratic South* (University of Georgia Press, 1963); V. O. Key, Jr., *Southern Politics* (Random House, 1949); and Robert Sherrill, *Gothic Politics in the Deep South* (Ballantine Books, 1969).

On the Stern Group and their challenge to taxes on political donations, see Jack Minnis, *Politics Is Business* (NOLA Express, Box 2342, New Orleans, Louisiana).

For accounts of the rapprochement between Northern Republicans and Southern Democrats in the last part of the nineteenth century, see C. Vann Woodward, *Reunion and Reaction* (Doubleday and Co., 1956); C. Vann Woodward, *The Origins of the New South, 1877–1913* (Louisiana State University Press, 1951); and Vincent P. DeSantis, *Republicans Face the Southern Question, 1877–1897* (Johns Hopkins Press, 1959).

For an old, but superb article on the South and Congress, see Marian Irish, "The Southern One-Party System and National Politics," *Journal of Politics* (February, 1942). The quote on page 92 comes from page 85 of this article. The quotation in the footnote on page 92 is from the reference book *Congress and the Nation, 1945–1964* (Congressional Quarterly Service, 1965, page 1412). On the voting patterns of Congressmen on various substantive issues, see David R. Mayhew, *Party Loyalty Among Congressmen* (Harvard University Press, 1966).

On machine Democrats and their alliance with the Southerners, see Norman C. Miller, "The Machine Democrats," *Washington Monthly* (June, 1970), from which two quotations are taken; Richard Bolling, *House Out of Order* (Dutton, 1965); and Richard Bolling, *Power in the House* (Dutton, 1968). On subsidy seeking in American politics, see Martin and Susan Tolchin, *To the Victor* . . . (Random House, 1971).

On the endurance of political machines, and representative quotes concerning the mythology of their demise, see Bruce M. Stave, "The New Deal and the Building of an Urban Political Machine: Pittsburgh, A Case Study," (Unpublished Ph.D. dissertation, University of Pittsburgh, 1966). The quote from Max Lerner on page 102, along with the refutation of it, are in Bernard F. Donahue, *Private Plans and Public Dangers* (University of Notre Dame Press, 1965, page 187).

On the Mississippi Challenge of 1971, see Robert Sherrill, "92nd Congress: Eulogy and Evasion," *The Nation* (February 15, 1971), and "Mississippi Challenge," *The New Republic* (January 16, 1971). The comments about Colmer on page 105 are from page 8 of *The New Republic* article.

The sources for other quotes found in this chapter are as follows: Pearson's comment on Senator McClellan, on page 80 of the text, appears in Drew Pearson and Jack Anderson's previously-cited *The Case Against Congress*, page 195; C. Vann Woodward's view on Northern Republican hopes for the South, on page 85 of the text, appears in his previously-cited *Reunion and Reaction,* page 104; the judgement of the unidentified person in South Carolina, which appears on page 89 of the text, is in V. O. Key's already-cited *Southern Politics,* page 150; the quote from Thomas E. Dewey on page 97 of the text is in V. O. Key, Jr., *Politics, Parties, and Pressure Groups* (Crowell Publishing Company, 1964, page 221); and the quotes from Robert Sherrill, Representative John Conyers, and Representative Abner Mikva, on pages 106 and 107 of the text, can be found in Robert Sherrill's previously-cited article in *The Nation* (February 15, 1971).

CHAPTER 4: LIMOUSINE LIBERALS

For a detailed history of Americans for Democratic Action, see Clifton Brock, *Americans for Democratic Action* (Public Affairs Press, 1962). For good accounts of the National Committee for an Effective Congress, see Harry M. Scoble, *Ideology and Electoral Action: A Comparative Case Study of the National Committee for an Effective Congress* (Chandler Publishing Company, 1967), and Neal Gregory, "Washington Pressures/the National Committee for an Effective Congress," *National Journal* (February 7, 1970).

On the details of the battle between Americans for Democratic Action and the Progressive Party in 1948, see Curtis D. MacDougall, *Gideon's Army,* Volumes I, II, and III (Marzani and Munsell, 1965). The judgment of the conflict quoted on page 120 of the text appears in Volume III, page 870; the judgment quoted on page 122 appears in Volume III, page 639. For an account of the battle which is based on ADA material, see Brock's already-cited

Americans for Democratic Action, which contains, on page 51, the comments by Chester Bowles cited on page 117 herein.

The task of "weighing" Communist influence in the *formation* of the Progressive Party is a difficult one. A exhaustive historical study of the problem has yet to be written. That there were Communists involved there is no doubt, as I said in the text. However, I believe their role was greatly exaggerated by those writing at the time, partly out of hysteria, partly out of a desire to see Henry Wallace badly defeated.

In making this judgment, I was persuaded by the evidence in the aforementioned three-volume work, *Gideon's Army.* I hope no one will call my view on this matter incorrect until he has dealt fairly with the *Gideon's Army* volumes, especially Chapters 12 and 13 of Volume I.

My view of this matter is not completely that of Mac-Dougall in *Gideon's Army,* however. I also was influenced by Karl Schmidt's *Henry A. Wallace Quixotic Crusade 1948* (Syracuse University Press, 1960), which concludes that the Communist role was greatly overstated. My inclination to accept MacDougall's evidence was tempered somewhat by an excellent review-essay on Schmidt's book by James Weinstein, "The Premature Crusade," *Studies on The Left* (Volume II, No. 1, 1961). Weinstein's major conclusion (page 104) on the importance of Communist influence is that "This is certainly true [that Wallace himself constituted the decisive factor in the determination that there was to be a third party in 1948], but it is equally true that without the Communists there could have been no Progressive Party in 1948, that they bear the responsibility for its organization. And although the Communists did not create Wallace or determine his program, they did do their best to create the impression of much greater organization support than actually existed."

The details of Clark Clifford's plan for the 1948 campaign are in Irwin Ross, *The Loneliest Campaign* (The New American Library, 1968). The ADA effort to draft Dwight Eisenhower for the Democratic presidential nomination in 1948 is recounted in the aforementioned book by Brock on the ADA.

The quote on pages 126–127 concerning the attempts by liberals to move the civil rights activists into voter registration drives is in Howard Zinn, *SNCC, The New Abolitionists* (Beacon Press, 1964, page 58). For information on foundation support of the civil rights struggle in the sixties, see Pat Watters and Reese Cleghorn, *Climbing Jacob's Ladder* (Harcourt, Brace, and World, 1967, pages 49 and 64). I also consulted foundation reports for such financial information.

For details on Mr. and Mrs. Stephen Currier and their liberal efforts, see Reese Cleghorn, "The Angels Are White: Who Pays the Bill for Civil Rights," *The New Republic* (August 17, 1963), from which the quotes on pages 128–29 are taken; Thomas P. Ronan, "Foundation Aids Fight by Negroes," *The New York Times* (August 4, 1963, page 61); "The Cities Own Pressure Group," *Business Week* (Oct. 1, 1966, page 158); and articles on the Curriers in *The New York Times* for January 19, January 26, February 1, and February 16, 1967.

The quotations from Paul Cowan concerning Al Lowenstein and the Mississippi Freedom Democratic Party (on pages 132 and 134) can be found in Paul Cowan, "What Makes Al Lowenstein Run?" *Ramparts* (September, 1968, page 48) and Paul Cowan, *The Making of an Un-American*

(Viking Press, 1970, page 50). Cowan's book is an incisive commentary on the limits of the liberal mentality in its dealings with less privileged people in this and other nations.

Fannie Lou Hamer's account of her discussion with Joseph Rauh and Hubert Humphrey, quoted on page 133 of the text, can be found in Robert Sherrill, "92nd Congress: Eulogy and Evasion," *The Nation* (February 15, 1971). The quote concerning Lowenstein and the liberal mentality (page 134) is in David Halberstam, "The Man Who Ran Against Lyndon Johnson," *Harper's Magazine* (December, 1968), page 50.

There is detailed information available on the financing of the McCarthy campaign. See especially Herbert E. Alexander, *Financing the 1968 Election* (D. C. Heath and Company, 1971).

My account of the Michigan Democratic Party follows John H. Fenton, *Midwest Politics* (Holt, Rinehart, and Winston, 1966). As Fenton says on pages 18–19: "However, the names of G. Mennen Williams, Hicks Griffiths, and Neil Staebler made the coalition safe and relatively respectable in the minds of many Michigan voters. The liberals, though, were not simply a facade for labor domination. In truth, they subsequently provided most of the ideological and formal leadership of the party. I also drew from Stephen and Vera Sarasohn, *Political Party Patterns in Michigan* (Wayne State University Press, 1957).

On the Wisconsin Democratic Party, see Fenton's *Midwest Politics* as well as David Adamany, *Financing Politics* (University of Wisconsin Press, 1969), and William Connelly, "Senator William Proxmire: What Makes Him Run?" *Science* (June 19, 1970). In giving great stress to the role of Proxmire in the resurgence of the Democratic Party in

Wisconsin, I relied on Fenton, page 56: "By almost universal consent in Wisconsin, the most important single person in the building of Wisconsin's Democratic Party was conceded to be William Proxmire."

The story of the "Berle Letter" which helped to bring money to Senator Proxmire's re-election campaign is told on pages 215–17 of Harry M. Scoble's previously-cited *Ideology and Electoral Action: A Comparative Case Study of the National Committee for an Effective Congress.*

On the importance of old-line rich in politics, see E. Digby Baltzell, *The Protestant Establishment* (Random House, 1964). For a good case study of the role of Republican-bred mavericks in the Democratic take-over of Philadelphia in the late forties and early fifties, see James Reichley, *The Art of Government* (Fund for the Republic, 1959).

CHAPTER 5: THE MISRULING OF AMERICA

The diagram on page 148 first appeared in my "How the Power Elite Set National Goals," which was reprinted in Kan Chen's *National Priorities* (San Francisco Press, 1970) and Robert Perrucci and Marc Pilisuk's *The Triple Revolution Emerging* (Little, Brown, and Company, 1971).

The comments on pages 150 and 151 concerning the role of the Council on Foreign Relations are from one of the few articles available on the group, Joseph Kraft's "School for Statesmen," *Harper's Magazine* (July, 1958). For a highly useful recent article that provides new evidence of the Council's importance, see J. Anthony Lukas, "The Council on Foreign Relations—Is It a Club? Seminar? Presidium? Invisible Government?" *The New York Times Magazine* (November 21, 1971).

For the role of Robert Lovett in the selection of Kennedy's cabinet members, see Arthur M. Schlesinger, Jr., *A Thousand Days* (Houghton Mifflin, 1965, pages 128–41). Schlesinger begins (page 128) by jocularly noting that Lovett was one of the "present leaders" of an "American Establishment" whose "front organizations" are the Rockefeller, Ford, and Carnegie foundations and the Council on Foreign Relations.

For details and references on the policy-planning groups, see Chapters Five and Six of *The Higher Circles*. I also discussed the importance of these groups in "The Power Elite," *The Center Magazine* (March, 1970) and in "Some Friendly Answers to Radical Critics," *The Insurgent Sociologist* (Spring, 1972). For an insightful case study of the role of such groups in foreign policy, see David Eakins, "Business Planners and America's Postwar Expansion," in David Horowitz, ed., *Corporations and the Cold War* (Monthly Review Press, 1969).

The quotations on pages 152 and 153 suggesting the minor role of political parties in policy formation can be found in Walter Dean Burnham, "Party Systems and the Political Process," *The American Party Systems* (Oxford University Press, 1967, pages 203–204).

Information on the Committee for Economic Development comes in great measure from two books by Karl Schriftgiesser, *Business Comes of Age* (Harper & Row, 1960) and *Business and Public Policy* (Prentice-Hall, 1967). The account of the Committee for Economic Development forum in San Francisco appeared in the San Francisco *Chronicle* (May 23, 1970), page 7.

As noted in the text, the best account of the ultra-conservative faction of the power elite is Wesley McCune, *Who's Behind Our Farm Policy* (Frederick A. Praeger,

1956). The Greenbrier Conferences are noted by McCune and by James Deakin, *The Lobbyists* (Public Affairs Press, 1966), and are more fully discussed by Donald R. Hall, *Cooperative Lobbying: The Power of Pressure* (University of Arizona Press, 1969).

On the differences between the Council on Foreign Relations-Committee for Economic Development mentality and the ultra-conservative National Association of Manufacturers outlook, see the just-cited books by Schriftgiesser as well as two articles by David S. McLellan and Charles E. Woodhouse, "The Business Elite and Foreign Policy," *Western Political Quarterly* (March, 1960) and "American Business Leaders and Foreign Policy: A Study in Perspectives," *The American Journal of Economics and Sociology* (July, 1966). An account of the spat over the CED-financed labor report appears in William F. Rickenbacker, "CED: Tycoon Trap?" *National Review* (February 26, 1963). This article, which was brought to my attention in a sociology term paper by Alex McTavish, is the source of the quote that appears on page 161. Schriftgiesser's *Business and Public Policy* also recounts this dispute and is the source of the quotation on page 162.

On the policy struggle in Congress, see again the information and references in Chapters Five and Six of *The Higher Circles,* as well as pages 346–53 of that book. Three informative articles on Common Cause are "Gardner's Cause," *Newsweek* (December 7, 1970); "Common Cause," *The New Republic* (March 20, 1971); and Saul Friedman, "Common Cause: Uncommon Response," *Los Angeles Times* (June 13, 1971, page G-2).

On the special businessmen's committees that oversee the functioning of the federal government, see Grant McConnell, *Private Power and American Democracy*

(Alfred A. Knopf, 1966) and Robert W. Dietsch, "The Invisible Bureaucracy: Government Committees Serving Private Interests," *The New Republic* (February 20, 1971). Dietsch's article is a brief summary of recent Congressional investigations.

The quotation on page 171 concerning retainer fees to the law firms of Congressmen appears in Drew Pearson and Jack Anderson's previously-cited *The Case Against Congress,* page 102.

John Kenneth Galbraith makes his case for working within the Democratic Party in *Who Needs the Democrats* (Doubleday and Co., 1970).

INDEX